Fine Art
Adventures

Fine Art Adventures

36 Creative, Hands-On Projects Inspired by Classic Masterpieces

MAJA PITAMIC AND JILL LAIDLAW

Introduction by Mike Norris, Metropolitan Museum of Art, USA

CHICAGO REVIEW PRESS

Contents

Art and Children
by Mike Norris

It's not news that parents and children are hard pressed to find the time to get to know each other better. If parents aren't spending most of the week commuting to work, working, then returning home, they are taking their children to a dizzying array of after-school activities. And, alluring new technologies have grown stronger and more numerous, reducing family time further. So what can a family do to play together, have fun together, and, in the process, learn about each other?

Fine Art Adventures is an answer. Art can bring parent and child together to learn and discuss, and the paintings in this book have a significant power to bring people together. This volume takes aim at the overwhelming desire of children to experiment with and manipulate materials to express themselves. The activities in *Fine Art Adventures* bring parents and children into a learning environment stocked with fun; they are calibrated to the expression of creativity, not pegged to the differing abilities of family members. One cannot, of course, ask a six-year-old child to be master of the materials and techniques of a famous oil painter. But the genius of this book is that each activity—designed for the skills of children aged between six and eight—extends logically from the original artwork, no matter what its medium, providing refreshing insights about painters and painting.

The carefully crafted activities do not ask family artists to slavishly copy works of art by using the same exact materials and techniques the original artists used. In keeping with the skill set of nonprofessional artists of varying ages, the activities use a wide variety of media that still manage to provide insights into the techniques and lives of the featured artists. Examples include producing three-dimensional versions of paintings and flip books inspired by artworks that are hundreds of years old. Some art activities serve as starting points for further projects, such as creating your own version of a portrait of Elizabeth I and then framing it, or making fruit out of newspaper and then drawing them in a still life study. All of the activities are manageble and fun, and all of them will enhance your family's enjoyment and understanding of art.

Mike Norris has been a staff educator at the Metropolitan Museum of Art for over fifteen years and oversees the teaching in the Met's programs for families at the Main Building in Manhattan.

Introduction by Maja Pitamic

Time after time I am bowled over by children's responses to paintings. They see with a directness and freshness that seems far removed from the world of art. On one occasion I was looking at Van Gogh's *Starry Night* with my class. I asked them why they thought Van Gogh had chosen to paint the sky in that particular way. After several very observant answers, a four-year-old girl put her hand up and said, "Because he wanted to show us how beautiful the world is." Countless books have been written about Van Gogh and yet a four-year-old can sum up in one sentence the purpose and intent of his paintings.

I hope that your children will similarly delight and amaze you with some of their responses to the paintings they see. Along the way you will also come to understand how they perceive the world around them by their responses. The art activities inspired directly from the paintings will allow your children to explore and develop their own creative skills and talents.

Fine Art Adventures will enable you to introduce the world of art to your child, but relax, no prior knowledge of the subject is needed. Each painting comes with a brief introduction, followed by suggestions for questions the painting may inspire and art activities. The art activities use materials that are readily available and they come with clear step-by-step instructions. You don't need to start at Chapter 1 and work your way through. Let your child choose which picture or activity appeals to them the most and work from there.

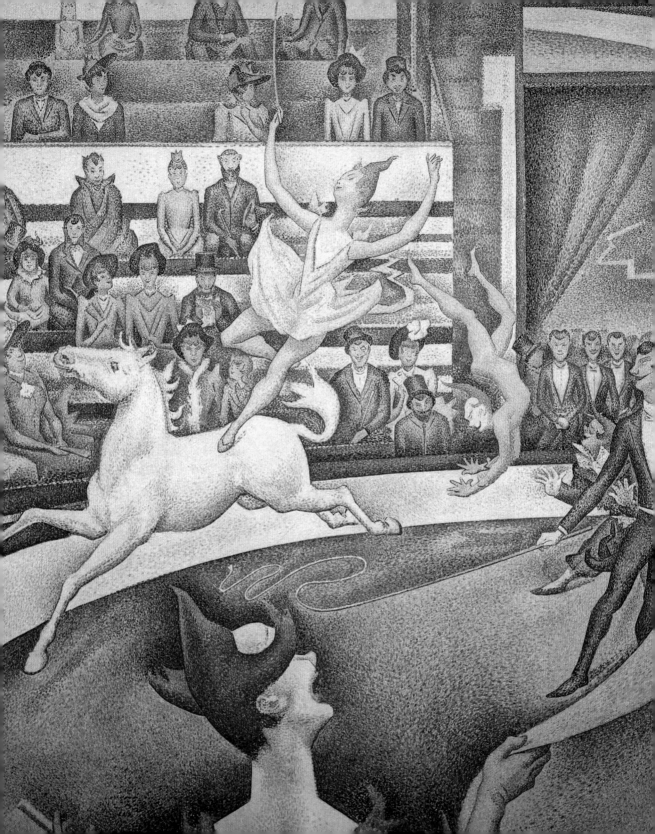

1 Color

Imagine a day without color. How different would
your life be? Color fills every part of our lives and so
we tend to take it for granted. Each color produces its
own set of moods and feelings. Yet colors don't just
work in isolation—when put alongside other colors
they can create a whole new drama and dynamism
of emotions. It is this that artists tap into when they
use color in their paintings. So in this chapter we have
the bold, intense blocks of color in Matisse's *The Snail*,
the primary colors, applied in dots, of Seurat's action
painting *The Circus*, and the subtle earth tones of
Lipunja's *Aboriginal Bark Painting*.

The Snail

If you had to choose only one artwork in the world to represent color then it would have to be Matisse's *The Snail*. Matisse has distilled the very essence of color into this picture. You may think that in creating an abstract (not realistic) work composed of a pattern of blocks of color there would be little to attract our attention. But you would be surprised how this picture reaches out to people, drawing them in and capturing their imagination.

Artist	Henri Matisse
Nationality	French
Painted	1953

What's the story?

To find the story behind this artwork you have to look at Matisse's life. The first thing to consider is the artwork's size; it measures just over 9 x 9 feet (2.7 x 2.7 m). You can pace this out on the floor. It's huge! The picture was produced on this scale not only for aesthetic reasons but for practical ones too. Matisse worked well into his 80s and had to battle with failing eyesight. *The Snail* was created a year before Matisse died and is on a monumental scale so that he could see the picture he was working on.

The blocks of color are torn pieces of paper painted with gouache paint. The blocks were arranged onto a white canvas by Matisse and his assistants. Look at the picture with half-closed eyes. You will discover that even with this limited view, the colors zing out of the canvas.

Matisse wanted to create art despite his physical limitations and this fact seems to intrigue people the most about this painting. If you want to understand Matisse's failing eyesight and his continuing desire to paint just think about any time you have wanted to do something new and the determination it has taken to achieve your goal.

Think about . . .

Why did Matisse use bright colors instead of snail-like colors?
Would this picture have had the same impact if it had been made with brown tones? Matisse was continually experimenting with color and how different colors make us feel.

Can you see the snail hiding in the picture?
Look very closely at the colored blocks. Do you see the small snail in the mauve block?

Why did Matisse choose a snail?
Perhaps for the beautiful shape of its spiral shell—it's such a dynamic shape, where does it start and where does it end?

Project: Tissue-paper picture

The main material used in this art activity is tissue paper. Tissue paper has the advantage of being very easy to tear and it also has a pleasing, tactile feel—when torn it has a wonderful raggedy edge.

1 Lay your ruler down on a piece of tissue. Tear the tissue into strips down the length of the ruler. These strips will be the border of your picture.

2 Now tear the tissue into about ten rough 4-inch (10-cm) squares. Make sure you have an even mix of colors.

3 Arrange the tissue-paper squares on the white heavy paper. Experiment with the position of the pieces of tissue until you are satisfied with the composition.

4 Use the glue stick to stick the tissue paper down. Don't stick the tissue paper completely down, leave some of the edges free—this gives an extra three-dimensional feel to your picture.

You will need

A ruler

A selection of brightly colored tissue paper

One sheet of 11 x 17 inch heavy white paper or larger if you want

A glue stick

Project: Color tones

By gradually adding more and more of a color
to white paint you can slowly darken it through
a series of tones.

1 Working horizontally, mark off the canvas at 1½-inch (4-cm) intervals using your pencil and ruler. Place the tape in a horizontal line below the first 1½-inch (4-cm) marking.

2 Put some white paint onto the plate and mix in the tiniest amount of your favorite color. Now apply the paint to the empty band of canvas above the masking tape.

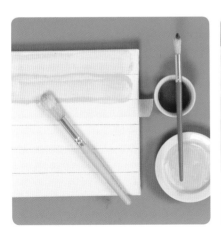

3 Move the masking tape down to the next 1½-inch (4-cm) mark.

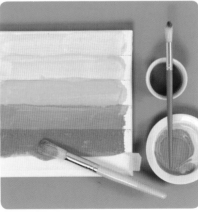

4 Add some more of your chosen color to the white paint to make a darker shade and then apply the paint to the next empty band of canvas. Continue until you reach the bottom of the canvas.

You will need

A mounted canvas, any size will do

A pencil

A ruler

A piece of masking tape slightly longer than the length of the canvas

White paint

Your favorite color of poster or acrylic paint

A plate for mixing the tones

A square-ended paintbrush, about 1 inch (2.5 cm) thick, plus another paintbrush for mixing the tones

Top tip

You might need a scratch piece of paper to try out the colors before you put them on the canvas.

The Circus

Seurat's painting of this circus scene captures that split second in time, that gasp of amazement from the crowd, as the dancer impossibly balances on the back of the pony and the acrobat is caught mid-tumble. The dynamic energy of the performers is contrasted with the stillness of the crowd. The overall impression of the painting is fantastical—like something remembered from a dream.

Artist	Georges Seurat
Nationality	French
Painted	1891

What's the story?

Born in Paris in 1859, Seurat trained at the École des Beaux-Arts and as a student he studied the scientific work of the chemist Michel Eugène Chevreul. Chevreul looked at optics and color and particularly at the division of light into primary colors (red, yellow, and blue). This was to form the basis of Seurat's painting style, known as Pointillism or, as he preferred to call it, Divisionism. Seurat put tiny dots of unmixed color next to each other on a white background so that from a distance they fuse together in the viewer's eye to give the appearance of other colors. As well as using a scientific basis for his exploration of color in painting, Seurat also tried to find scientific ways of painting the most harmonious lines.

The Circus was Seurat's final work. Considered unfinished, *The Circus* combined his interest in both color and line. We are in a ringside seat, getting only a glimpse of the blurred faces of the performers as they speed past, similar to the image a camera takes as it captures moving objects. The echoing shapes of the performers' bodies, the use of the orange tones, which link the audience and performers together, and the yellow scarf the clown holds, leads your eye out of the picture and then pulls you back in again. Seurat's use of color and line are a balancing act as poised as the dancer on the back of the pony.

Think about . . .

Why did Seurat apply the paint in dots of pure color?
He wanted to reproduce colors as they appear in nature, something artists of earlier generations had been attempting to do. It's our eyes that blend individual colors together.

The performers link up to make a diamond shape. What effect does this have on the painting?
The diamond shape unifies the painting. The shapes are echoed and repeated—the figure of the acrobat is repeated in the figure of the ringmaster, which is further emphasized by the scarf that wraps around him.

Project: Spray picture

This art project recreates Pointillism using stencils and paint. The paint is applied by using a toothbrush and flicking the bristles. The paint is laid on in individual colors which build up to produce a final unified effect.

1 Begin by creating your stencils. Sketch the circus figures onto your posterboard. You can trace the characters from Seurat's painting on page 17 or create some of your own. Cut them out and set aside.

2 On your plain paper sketch out the circus ring, doorway, and rows of seating. Use the masking tape and cut out strips to cover these areas.

You will need

A sheet of white posterboard for the stencils

A pencil

A pair of scissors

A sheet of white heavy paper, any size

Masking tape

An old toothbrush

Ready mixed or powder paint in orange, yellow, red, and blue

A paintbrush for mixing

A ruler, or you could use your finger

3 Arrange the stencils on the plain paper and get all of your paints ready. Dip your toothbrush in the yellow paint and hold it over the paper. Pull your ruler or finger across the bristles towards you—this will make the paint spray away from you. Move the toothbrush around the paper so that the paint is evenly applied.

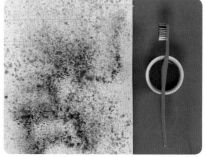

4 Clean your toothbrush and repeat step 3 with another color. Keep working this way until you have used all your colors. Use strong colors, like orange, with care as they can overpower the painting. When you are using a darker color look at how Seurat used dark colors to create shadows around the figures. When the paint is dry, carefully remove the masking tape and the stencils.

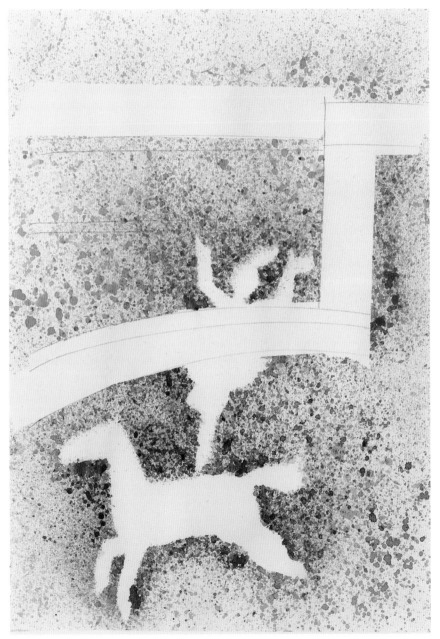

Top tips

• Try the toothbrush spray action on a piece of scratch paper before using it on your painting.
• Make sure you keep the stencils still while you apply the paint.
• Don't overload the toothbrush or it will drip.
• Work slowly and keep checking that there is an even balance between all the colors.

Project: Dot picture

This is the cheater's version of Pointillism because it imitates the style of Pointillism without any of the hard work. Fine sandpaper and wax crayons are used to make the original picture, and then it is transferred onto plain paper using a lukewarm iron. The texture of the sandpaper is picked up by the transfer and gives the impression of Pointillism.

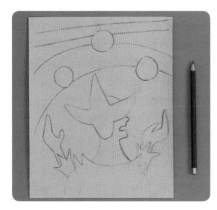

You will need

A sheet of fine sandpaper, roughly 8½ x 11 inch (Letter) size

A pencil

Assorted wax crayons

A sheet of 8½ x 11 inch (Letter) white heavy paper

A lukewarm iron

1 With the pencil, lightly and roughly sketch out your circus scene on the piece of sandpaper. You may want to try out a few ideas first on a piece of scratch paper.

2 When you are happy with your drawing begin to color it in using your wax crayons. Press quite hard when you are coloring and make sure that no bits of sandpaper show through as this will affect the quality of the finished picture.

3 Place your finished sandpaper picture face up onto an ironing board. Put a plain piece of paper over the top. With an adult, iron over the top of the plain paper with a lukewarm iron.

4 Lift up the plain piece of paper and you will find that your sandpaper picture has been magically transferred onto the plain paper.

Aboriginal Bark Painting

In Lipunja's abstract painting representing the body there aren't any dazzling blocks of color, such as you would see in a work by an artist like Henri Matisse. The colors Lipunja used came from his world and landscape—earth tones, reds, whites, and ochre. Lipunja demonstrated that subdued colors, when subtly used, can be just as compelling as bright primary colors. You could have found this painting in the chapter in this book on shape as well as here, in color, because there is complete harmony between the colors used and the composition.

Artist	Lipunja
Nationality	Aboriginal Australian
Painted	c.1960s

What's the story?

We know very little about Lipunja because for him, and other Aboriginal artists, his art was not about individual fame but about a celebration of the whole of Aboriginal life. Lipunja painted all that was dear and sacred to him—earth, water, animals, and the worship of ancestor spirits.

Aboriginal art came to be known in America and Europe during the earlier part of the 20th century and there is evidence that Pablo Picasso was influenced by it. Lipunja and his fellow artists from Arnhem Land came to prominence during the 1960s and their work is now exhibited in galleries around the world.

Lipunja's studio was probably outside and the materials he used were taken from the natural world. Instead of a canvas he used a piece of bark so the picture has a wonderful texture that makes the paint seem to shimmer. There is perfect balance between the shapes, which creates a sense of movement. Perhaps the most appealing aspect of this painting is the sense of timelessness that it conveys. The colors and shapes used are as old as the Aboriginal peoples themselves—perhaps this is why Lipunja's painting is truly great.

Think about . . .

Why did Lipunja draw the human body in this way?
Aboriginal artists use symbols to represent figures, animals, and the landscape, such as a wavy line that stands for running water.

How was the bark prepared?
A section of bark would have been taken from the tree and the outer bark removed. The inner "skin" was then smoothed and sanded down. The bark was then weighed down to flatten it.

How was the paint put on?
With feathers, chewed-up bits of bark, and twigs.

"This picture makes me happy because it's got so much sun in it."

Tilly, age 5

Project: Tie-dye sunburst

Aboriginals don't just use painting as a way of expressing their art but also as a way of decorating everyday objects. So in this art project we are going to use tie-dye to create a sunburst design on a fabric square that can be used as decoration—you could do several of these fabric squares in different colors and then join them together to make a patchwork wall hanging or cushion covers. Tie-dye is probably one of the oldest methods of fabric printing.

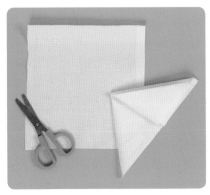

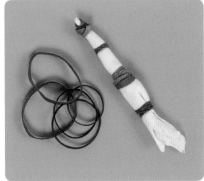

1 Cut your fabric into a square, then fold it into quarters. Squeeze it down so that it looks like a closed umbrella. Tightly secure a rubber band around the open end of the fabric.

2 Evenly space the rest of the rubber bands down the fabric in the same way. The dye won't penetrate the fabric where the rubber bands are tight.

3 Put enough water in the bucket to cover the fabric and mix in the food coloring—how much depends on how strong you want the color to be. Wear gloves as dyes tend to leave permanent stains. Put the fabric into the bucket of dye and make sure that it is covered with the liquid.

4 You may need to use your tongs to push the fabric down so that it absorbs the liquid. Soak the fabric for several hours or overnight, then take it out of the dye. Throw away the dyed water and wash the bucket to prevent staining. Allow the fabric to dry out. Iron the fabric on a low heat, then stand back and admire your work.

Top tip

Aborigines use natural dyes. If you want to use natural dyes, you could try any of the following: Beets, tea in bags, spinach, onion skins, or berries.

Project: Textures with paint

Try your hand at painting your own Aboriginal-style painting. Use a cardboard comb to create the textural feel of the bark. Then layer a pattern over the top with some white paint.

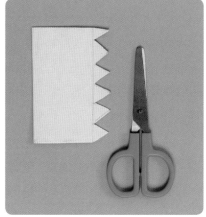

1 Draw a small zigzag line across your cardboard rectangle then cut along it. This is your paint comb.

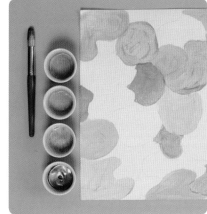

2 Apply the paint to the white heavy paper using a paintbrush. Create a random pattern but lock the colors together, like the pieces of a jigsaw puzzle.

You will need

A small cardboard rectangle

A pencil

A pair of scissors

A sheet of white heavy paper, any size

A selection of poster or acrylic paints in earth shades, white, and brown

Medium- and thin-sized paintbrushs

A white or light-colored pencil

Scratch paper

A pencil

A toothpick or pencil

3 While the paint is still wet, take your paint comb and drag it across the paper. Don't worry if it's not perfectly straight, it will look more natural if it has a slight wave to it.

4 Draw a design on the scratch paper with your pencil—the same one as Lipunja or something new. Then take a white or light-colored pencil and sketch your design onto your dry painted paper.

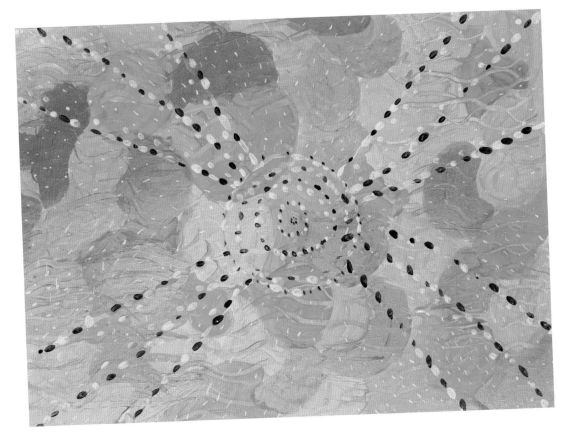

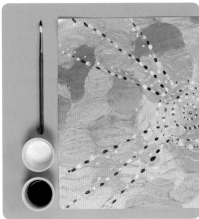

5 Take your white and dark brown paints and paint them over the top of your design.

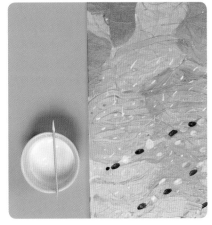

6 Before the paint is dry use a toothpick to mark the paint in tiny left and right diagonals. This imitates the rough texture of Lipunja's bark painting.

Top tip

Apply the paint comb very lightly so that the grooves do not go too deep.

2 Black & white

Black and white—are they actually colors or tones or shades? This argument has been going on for centuries and we still haven't arrived at a definitive answer. But one thing is certain, black, whether a color or a tone, follows a completely different set of optical rules than all the other colors. White also has special characteristics. One would think that working with just black and white would restrict an artist but, as the selection of pictures for this chapter demonstrates, it seems to stimulate and challenge artists' imaginations.

Portrait of Bernhard von Reesen

In Dürer's *Portrait of Bernhard von Reesen*, black and white paint has been used to create a portrait of elegant simplicity. There is nothing to distract your eye so the entire focus of your attention is drawn to the sitter's face. In this portrait's very simplicity, Dürer reveals his skill as a draftsman and as a painter in oils.

Artist	Albrecht Dürer
Nationality	German
Painted	1521

What's the story?

Albrecht Dürer helped to transform the status of the artist from artisan to wealthy professional who commanded a workshop of assistants and whose patrons (customers) included kings and emperors. Dürer was filled with curiosity and this is reflected in the incredible diversity of his work, which covered everything from engravings to altarpieces, nature studies, landscapes, portraits, and works on the proportions of the human body.

Born in 1471, Dürer was the son of a goldsmith and was trained in woodcutting and printing. Dürer was a supreme draftsman and it is this skill that shines out in *Portrait of Bernhard von Reesen*—every line counts, nothing is superfluous. Dürer settled in Nuremberg, Germany, where he opened a workshop staffed with assistants so that he could cope with the huge number of commissions he received. While working on these commissions Dürer perfected his technique of working in oil paints and this is possibly the greatest strength of this image. Dürer painted Bernhard's clothes with bold dynamic brushstrokes, saving all the fine detail for his face, which is framed by his hat and its shadow. Dürer recorded in his diary that "he made a portrait of Bernhart von Resten in oils" for which he was paid 8 florins. Sadly, Bernhard died only eight months later of the plague.

Think about . . .

Why did Dürer paint this portrait mostly in black and white?
By using a limited range of colors Dürer focused our attention on the sitter's face which, by contrast, is drawn in great detail. The use of just black and white also indicates that Bernhard is a serious and learned person, something that is emphasized further by the letter that Bernhard holds in his hand—during this time only members of the church and rich people were able to read and write.

Project: Three-dimensional portrait

This project concentrates on the line of a portrait rather than its color. Using glue you can make a three-dimensional, raised image. Then you can paint it gold and rub it with black shoe polish to create an antique look.

1 Lightly draw or trace Dürer's portrait of Bernhard onto your white card. If you can't see through the card then use tracing paper or greaseproof paper to trace the image (see Top Tips). When you are happy with your drawing go over it neatly and clearly with your pencil.

2 Test your glue on a scratch paper to check that it's running smoothly and evenly. Carefully go over your pencil lines with the glue until all the pencil lines have been covered. Be careful to lift your glue up quickly when you have completed a line to avoid any drips.

You will need

A pencil

A sheet of thick white card stock or thick paper and a piece of cardboard glued together

Tracing paper or greaseproof paper

White glue in a container with a nozzle top

Scratch paper

Gold acrylic paint or poster paint

A medium-sized paintbrush

Black shoe polish

Soft cloth

3 At this point you might want to add some extra details like the folds of the shirt or curls of the hair. Let the glue dry overnight and then paint all over the picture with the gold paint.

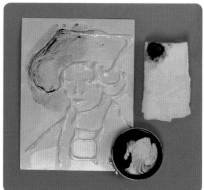

4 When the gold paint is dry put some black shoe polish on a soft cloth and rub it all over the picture to give it an antique look.

Top tips

Here's how to transfer an image using tracing paper:

• Trace the image you want to copy using a pencil and some tracing paper or greaseproof baking paper.

• Flip the tracing paper and go over the lines of the portrait on the other side with your pencil.

• Turn the tracing paper back over again and put it on the card or paper you want to transfer the image to.

• Go over the lines of the portrait one more time—this will transfer the image.

Project: Rubber-band printing

This activity uses rubber bands to create a simple printing technique. This project gets its inspiration from the fact that Albrecht Dürer was an engraver.

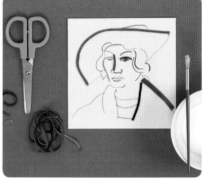

1 Start by drawing your portrait onto the cardboard (see Top Tips on page 33). You can use either Dürer's portrait on page 31 or your own design. Go over your pencil drawing with a ballpoint pen.

2 Measure and cut up pieces of both thicknesses of rubber band to fit over the lines of your drawing. Apply a generous layer of white glue with the brush. Make sure the rubber is securely stuck onto the cardboard and leave it to dry.

You will need

A square sheet of medium-thickness cardboard, 6 x 6 inches (15 x 15 cm)

A pencil

Tracing paper

A ballpoint pen

White glue

A medium-sized paintbrush

Thick and thin rubber bands

A pair of scissors

A sponge cloth

White ready-mixed paint or poster paint

A newspaper

A sheet of white heavy paper—the size will depend on how many you make

Tissue paper, different colors, cut into squares 6 x 6 inches (15 x 15 cm)

Glue stick

3 Using your brush, put some white paint onto your sponge cloth.

4 Press the cardboard picture onto the white paint (rubber-band-side down) and press all across the back. Lift off your picture and place it face-up onto a folded newspaper. Choose a tissue square and put it on top of the cardboard. Press lightly. Lift off gently.

5 Repeat step 4 again and again using different colors of tissue. Keep repeating this step until you have enough prints to fill your sheet of heavy paper.

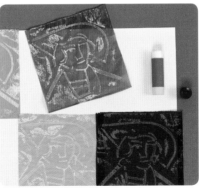

6 When the squares of tissue are dry, use the glue stick to stick them down onto the heavy paper to create a checkerboard effect.

Top tips

• Wash your brush right after using the white glue.
• Once you have put the paint onto the sponge cloth work quickly before the paint dries.
• You could try using black or different colored paints for the prints instead of white.

Buffel, Buffle

If you had to choose an animal to represent the United States then it would have to be the buffalo—it reminds us of the wide, open spaces of the Great Plains and the ancestry of the Plains Indians. In its strength and size, the buffalo represents a country that through its pioneering spirit has become the most powerful in the world. Yet in many ways this engraving of a buffalo makes many references to European art.

Artist	Jakob van der Schley
Nationality	Dutch
Painted	c.1770

What's the story?

Jakob van der Schley was not a major artist but I have chosen to feature his work because his art tells us a lot about his time. For centuries most art in Europe was specially commissioned by a wealthy customer, called a patron, but during the 18th century the rising merchant classes wanted to show off their new wealth and education and they did so by buying art and books lavishly illustrated with engravings.

 Engraving was a popular process because it allowed images to be copied in fine detail and then reproduced in large numbers. As Europeans went to explore the New World, there was a huge demand for pictures of what they had seen there. Van der Schley responded with his engravings of animals, such as the buffalo. But if you look at the countryside in this engraving it looks more like a Dutch landscape than the American plains. Similarly, the buffalo resembles a minotaur, the monster of Greek legend. Having a Classical education (knowledge of Greek and Roman art and literature) was essential for every gentleman so someone who bought a van der Schley engraving was showing that they were a person of taste. Although *Buffel, Buffle* is an image of the New World, it is also reassuringly European.

Think about . . .

Why did van der Schley choose to depict a buffalo in his engraving? The buffalo represents the New World, as America was called then. Europeans were eager to learn about these newly discovered lands and their plants and animals.

Who do you think would buy an engraving by van der Schley? The new moneyed classes bought engravings—they had made their fortunes through trade and industry and were keen to show off their wealth and status. To show themselves as men of learning their libraries would house images of the New World.

BUFFLE.

BUFFEL.

"The buffalo looks like it's dancing."

Noah, age 6

Project: Cave painting

This activity draws its inspiration from prehistoric cave paintings—a buffalo would be a very typical subject for such a painting. But relax, you don't have to find some suitable prehistoric cave to do this project, just grab some spackling paste and paint.

1 Start by mixing up the spackling paste. Fill the tray and then set it aside for a couple of hours, until it's hard.

2 Mix up your paint for the background. Brown earth tones would be appropriate. Apply the paint to the dry plaster and allow to dry.

You will need

A styrofoam tray (the type of tray that meat comes in), any size

Enough spackling paste to fill the tray

Poster, watercolor, or powder paints

A medium-sized paintbrush

Scratch paper

A pencil

A thin paintbrush

A sheet of fine sandpaper

Watered-down white glue or a beaten egg (optional)

A thick paintbrush

3 Take your pencil and do a practice sketch of your buffalo (trace the outline of van der Schley's engraving on page 37 or draw a buffalo of your own). Lightly draw in any other background details, such as trees.

4 Now draw your buffalo design in pencil onto the painted plaster. Paint in the buffalo and any other details you want to include. Allow to dry.

5 Take your sandpaper and lightly sand over the painting to give it an aged appearance.

6 You might want to glaze the painting—this will add a sheen to the painting and help to protect it. You can make a glaze by using watered-down white glue or a beaten egg. Apply either substance with a brush and allow to dry. Remove the styrofoam tray and display your cave painting.

Top tips

• Take time when mixing up your colors to create rich earth tones.
• Make sure that the buffalo stands out against the background and does not blend in too much.
• For this project, I prefer to use watercolor or powder paints because they can give a great variety of color tones.

Project: Buffalo painting

This art project relates to the indigenous people of the North American plains. The buffalo was integral to these peoples' way of life. We are going to use fabric stained to imitate the color of buffalo hide. We will use a wooden frame as a reference to the way buffalo hides would have been stretched out to dry.

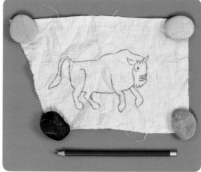

1 Ask an adult to make a pot of tea. When the tea has cooled, pour it into a container. Scrunch up your fabric and soak it in the tea for a couple of hours. Remove the fabric from the tea and allow it to dry.

2 Stretch out the fabric and weigh down the corners. Sketch out your buffalo in pencil. You could trace van der Schley's engraving on page 37 or you can do your own drawing.

Top tips

• Don't choose yarn that is too fat or you won't be able to get it through the eye of the needle.
• Remember to secure the wool at the end.
• Remember to choose natural colors for your leaf prints.

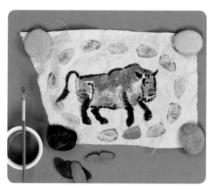

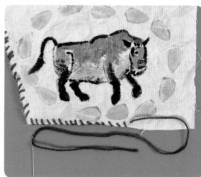

3 Paint in your buffalo and allow it to dry. Take a leaf and paint it using your chosen color. To ensure you have an even coverage of paint, do a test print on a bit of scrap paper. Press the leaf down and then lift it from the paper. Make a border of leaf prints around the buffalo and allow the paint to dry.

4 Thread and knot a length of yarn, then sew a border using an over stitch. Not only is this sewing decorative but it prevents the fabric from fraying.

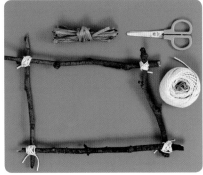

5 Make a frame with the sticks, overlapping them at the corners. Secure each corner with string. Once the frame is secure you may want to cover the string using raffia to give it a more natural look.

6 Cut four lengths of yarn, each about 16 inches (40 cm) long. These are your corner ties. Thread a length and sew it into the corner of the fabric, then cut away so that you have two lengths for tying. Repeat at each of the other corners. Tie and secure each corner onto the frame. Your picture is now ready to be displayed.

You will need

A piece of cotton or muslin cloth, 8½ x 11 inches (Letter) in size

Teabags

A plastic container

A pencil

Poster paints in earth tones

A variety of leaves for printing

Thin yarn

One large-eyed needle

Four sticks, two about 16 inches (40 cm) in length and two about 8 inches (20 cm) in length

String

Scissors

Raffia (optional)

3 Shape

No one would argue with the fact that shapes do not change their properties. A square will always have four equal sides, a triangle will have three sides of equal or unequal length. But as the next two paintings demonstrate (produced within three years of each other), pictures may have a common theme but they can look startlingly different. To see what I mean, take a look at Theo van Doesburg's simple tonal *Composition in Gray*, and Kazimir Malevich's hard-edged *Suprematist Composition*.

Composition in Gray

In Theo van Doesburg's painting *Composition in Gray*, sometimes called *Rag-time*, there are no figures, no story, no colors, just tones of gray and an arrangement of shapes. Yet this image catches our attention, making us think and reflect.

Artist	Theo van Doesburg
Nationality	Dutch
Painted	1919

What's the story?

Theo van Doesburg joined a group of young Dutch artists to produce a journal in 1917 called *De Stijl* (meaning "the style"). In this journal they set out their ideas on art and De Stijl also became the name of their art movement, although it is also known as Neo-Plasticism. De Stijl paintings featured horizontal and vertical lines and used black, white, and primary colors. De Stijl artists thought that art should be represented in as exact a way as math. De Stijl ideas also applied to architecture, furniture, and decorative objects like plates and fabrics.

For van Doesburg the De Stijl movement was also about changing the role of the artist in society and he thought that architecture should play an important part in achieving this. You only have to look at *Composition in Gray* to see the link van Doesburg made between art and architecture because the picture appears to be constructed of building blocks. The way van Doesburg shaded the painting in tones of gray created drama in the picture. Every time I look at this painting it suggests different things to me: the stones of an ancient culture, doorways opening onto unknown paths, and, in the sections of circles and ovals, a piece of the Milky Way.

The painting's alternative title, *Rag-time*, suggests a further link between Neo-Plasticism and math. Music, like math, follows a strict beat and pattern. Whistler (page 98) also saw a link between art and music and van Doesburg's work is almost the next step in Whistler's theories on art.

Think about . . .

Why did van Doesburg choose not to use any color in his painting?
Van Doesburg felt that using color would detract from the beauty of the shapes. He used tones of gray to bring out the form of the shapes and to give them a structural, three-dimensional quality.

Why did van Doesburg give the painting the alternative title of *Rag-time*?
Music, like math, has a regular time and beat so van Doesburg was stressing the ordered nature of his painting by naming it after a type of jazz music.

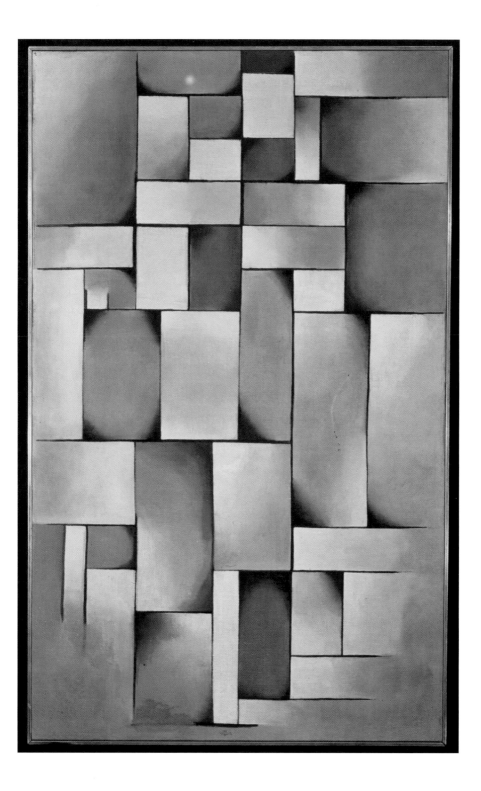

Project: Dramatic sculpture

This project turns van Doesburg's *Composition in Gray* into a three-dimensional sculpture and uses a desk lamp to add dramatic light and shadow effects.

1 Start by arranging and assembling your containers into a shape. When you are happy with your arrangement, glue together the pieces. Allow the glue to dry and set—this can take several hours.

You will need

Small empty containers like matchboxes, plastic cups, and paper towels tubes

White glue

White acrylic paint

A large paintbrush

A desk lamp or a flashlight

Black acrylic paint

A medium paintbrush

An old plate for mixing the paint

2 Paint your sculpture all over in white acrylic paint. You might need to do more than one coat; the main thing to do is to cover up any signs of the packaging beneath.

3 After the white paint has dried, take the desk lamp and shine it onto your sculpture. If you are using a flashlight it might be a good idea to rest it on some books. The shadows should be very clear. Find the darkest shadow and try to match its color by mixing up your paint to that shade. Apply the paint to those areas. Now find the next lightest tone, mixing your paint to match the tone and adding it to the sculpture. Keep repeating this step until all the tones of the shadows have been painted in. Now display your sculpture.

Top tips

- Be inventive with the way you arrange your containers. Don't just line them up, face-on, but put them at odd angles or cut up the tubes and place them sideways so that you can see the circles they make.
- You may want to use more than one light to create more dramatic light effects.
- Take time to mix up the correct color shades—it really helps to create the final effect.

Project: weaving with paper

This art project captures the sculptural, three-dimensional quality of van Doesburg's painting by making a paper loom using corrugated cardboard. The corrugated paper has a textured, raised surface that creates its own sense of movement, light, and shade. The loom is woven with paper strips in different shades of gray.

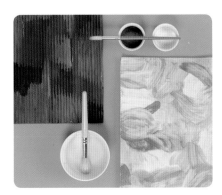

1 Start by making the heavy paper wet with your big paintbrush. While the paper is still wet, cover the surface in shades of gray. Leave the painted paper to dry. Do the same with the corrugated paper but do not wet the paper first. Allow this to dry.

2 Measure and mark off a 1½-inch (4-cm) border around the corrugated cardboard. Then measure and mark off vertical strips every ½ inch (1.25 cm) from the top of the border to the bottom. Starting at the top, cut along the marked out lines; stop when you get to the bottom border.

You will need

A sheet of 8½ x 11 inch (Letter) white heavy paper

Paintbrushes, thick and thin

Black and white poster paints or watercolor paint

A sheet of corrugated cardobard, 8½ x 11 inch (Letter) or larger

A ruler

A white pencil

A pair of scissors

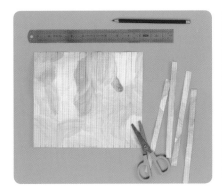

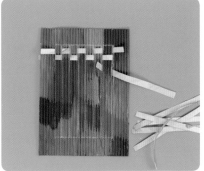

3 Measure and mark off ½-inch (1.25-cm) horizontal lines on the heavy paper, then cut into strips.

4 Take a cut strip and, in an over-and-under action, weave through the corrugated paper. Keep repeating this with new strips until you reach the bottom. Adjust the strips so that they are even on both sides and there are no gaps between the strips.

Top tips

• As you are weaving you may need to nudge the paper strips down to fill in any gaps.
• Make sure that you stick to the over-and-under action and remember not to skip over more than one vertical section.

Suprematist Composition

Kazimir Malevich's art propels us into the world of 20th-century painting with a force that is breathtaking in its inventiveness. In Malevich's pictures all references to the history of painting have been swept away. Every element of Malevich's paintings are pared down in order to announce the arrival of the new age of industrialism and technology.

Artist	Kazimir Malevich
Nationality	Russian
Painted	1915

What's the story?

Kazimir Malevich was born in Kiev (modern-day Ukraine) in 1878. He studied at the Moscow Institute of Painting, Sculpture and Architecture from 1904 to 1910. After 1910 his painting changed and developed into the style that became known as Suprematism. Suprematism was a version of Cubism. In Cubist paintings everyday objects were broken down into basic shapes, taken apart, and put back together again in a slightly disjointed way. Malevich showed his geometric Suprematist paintings to the public in Petrograd, Russia, in 1915. In these paintings he tried to make geometric shapes represent feelings or sensations. He also looked at developing the Suprematist style in three-dimensional models of buildings and this is very obvious when we look at this painting—the geometric shapes have a sculptural feel, as if you could reach out and grab hold of them. The sharp-edged, flat shapes seem to be welded together. He used bold primary colors and black to add to the painting's hard-edged atmosphere. The whole composition is made up of straight lines. Yet, despite the solid quality of the central shapes, the thin slivers of rectangles seem to fly away at random; this creates a feeling of movement so that the whole structure looks like a plane about to take off.

Think about . . .

If different colors had been used in the picture would it have mattered?
Cover up the black and see how this changes the painting. The green and black in the middle of the picture weigh down the large shapes there. If you painted these three shapes in light colors they would look as though they were floating away, not anchored down.

What would happen if you put circles into this painting?
The picture would look less rigid and the structural feel of the image would be lost.

1   Start by tracing the outlines of the shapes in the painting (page 51) onto your cardboard. Cut out the cardboard shapes and paint them on one side. When the painted side is dry, paint the other side.

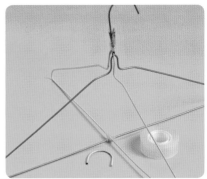

4   Take one of the coat hangers and have an adult cut away the hook with the pliers. Now insert one hanger through the other at a right angle to form a cross. Tape the hangers together at the point where they meet along the bottom and at the top, below the hook.

Project: Mobile sculpture

How can we recreate the sculptural feel of Malevich's painting? How can we recreate Malevich's floating shapes? The answer is to make a three-dimensional hanging mobile sculpture.

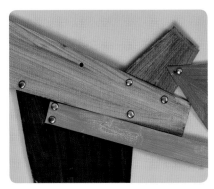

2 Assemble the pieces and mark with a pencil where you need an adult to make the holes for the paper fasteners. Pin the shapes together and make a hole in the biggest card shape (the green section). This is where your sculpture will hang from.

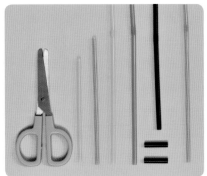

3 Now cut the straws into a variety of different lengths.

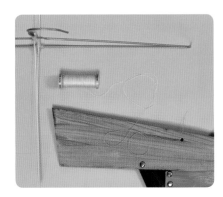

5 Attach some cotton thread (about 8 inches [20 cm] long) to the biggest cardboard section through the pre-made hole. Now tie the thread to the crossbar of the hangers.

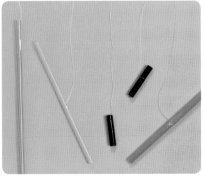

6 Cut threads between 8 inches (20 cm) and 16 inches (40 cm) long to match the number of straws. Tape a length of thread onto each straw so that some of the straws will hang vertically and some horizontally. Tie the straws along the crossbars of the hangers. Now you can hang up your mobile.

You will need

A large piece of thick cardboard, an old supermarket box or shoebox is ideal

A piece of tracing paper or greaseproof paper

A pencil

A pair of scissors

Poster or acrylic paints in the same colors as the painting or your own choice

A medium-sized paintbrush

Six paper fasteners

About six brightly colored straws

Two wire coat hangers (triangular in shape)

Pliers

Tape

Cotton thread

Project: Color blending

This art activity recreates the light, floating quality of the color blocks in Malevich's painting by using paint on wet paper—this makes the colors run and blend together.

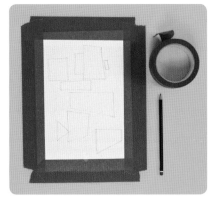

1 Start by sticking your paper onto your board or onto a clean table top with the masking tape. If you are using a table top make sure that the tape will not leave a mark when it is removed. Lightly sketch in where you want your blocks of color to go.

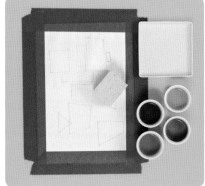

2 Wet your sponge and wring out any extra water, then drag the sponge across the paper in broad horizontal strokes so that the whole page becomes wet.

You will need

A sheet of 8½ x 11 inch (Letter) or larger white watercolor paper or heavy paper

A board larger than the paper, or a clean table top

Masking tape

A pencil

A sponge

Watercolor paints or powder paints

A thin- to medium-sized paintbrush

3 Now start filling in the blocks of color, remembering to clean your brush every time you use a new color.

4 When the paper and paint are dry, take the paper off the board or table top. You may like to go on to do a series of these paintings using a different combination of colors within the same shapes for each one.

4 Animals

Animals are possibly one of the most popular subjects in art, from the earliest cave paintings of prehistory right through to the present day. Animals have been recorded in every type of medium: in sculpture, on canvas, in wood, on ceramics, and in tapestries. The paintings and activities in this chapter reflect this breadth and diversity of subject matter and medium. Included here are Rousseau's iconic *Surprised!* and George Stubbs's masterful *A Couple of Foxhounds*.

Surprised!

Think of all the pictures that have been painted of animals and *Surprised!*, Henri Rousseau's painting of a tiger in a storm, is surely one of the most popular. What's the secret of the painting's enduring appeal? I think the answer is that if you had never seen a photograph of a jungle, this is probably how you would hope it would look—an exotic location, a dramatic storm, and of course a tiger. All these elements are combined in a powerful and bold way to create an image that once seen is never forgotten.

Artist	Henri Rousseau
Nationality	French
Painted	1891

What's the story?

Rousseau claimed that he had experience in the jungle from his time as a regimental guardsman in Mexico with the French Army, but when he was in the army he never left France. His jungle picture was created from plant studies he made at the botanical gardens, prints by other artists, and his imagination.

Rousseau had no art training and he painted the jungle with a simple, naïve quality. But this style adds to the drama, giving the picture a raw, direct energy.

Rousseau saw the jungle as if through a child's eye. Great big green glossy leaves frame the crouching tiger, who is ready to spring. For the final touch of drama a streak of lightning cuts through the dark storm clouds. The drama and emotion of the scene is heightened because there appears to be a conflict between nature and the tiger. The tiger digs in his claws to maintain his position against the full force of the wind. His body position tells us that he senses the danger but refuses to be cowed by it and, in a final act of defiance, he bares his teeth at the flash of lightning. Maybe it is this aspect of the painting that appeals most to people—the tiger standing firm against the odds.

Think about . . .

How did Rousseau manage to get such a sense of movement into the picture?
By painting all the trees and plants of the jungle in strong diagonals from left to right. The tiger's body is also a diagonal but it is rigid with his claws dug in to maintain his position against the wind—reinforcing the obvious strength of the storm.

How important is the lightning?
It adds to the tension and drama of the scence, highlighting the force of the storm. Apart from the tiger's teeth, the lightning is the only place where white paint has been used.

"The tiger looks really scared—I'd help him out of the forest."

Holly, age 6

Project: Jungle box

With nothing more than an old shoebox, this activity re-creates Rousseau's *Surprised!* in a three-dimensional format. The shoebox works on the same principal as a pinhole camera and gives you a clearer understanding of how objects can look small or large depending on their distance from the viewer.

1 Cut out the top of the box lid in a rectangular shape, leaving a border of about 1 inch (2.5 cm).

4 When the paint is dry, arrange the soil, pebbles, and plants inside the box, holding them in place with Sticky Tack.

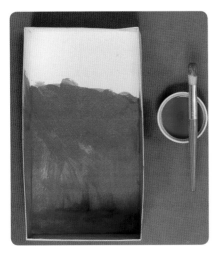

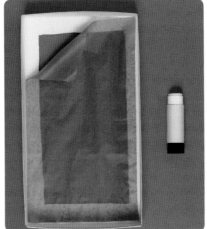

2 Paint the inside of the box. While the paint is drying, measure a piece of tissue paper to fit the box lid.

3 Run the glue stick along the border inside the box lid and stick down the prepared tissue paper.

5 Make a small peep hole at one end of the box with the point of your scissors. Paint a streak of lightning at the other end of the box on the inside.

6 Place the tiger in your jungle scene and put the lid on the box. View the scene through the hole. Experiment with the position of the tiger to see how it affects the image.

You will need

A shoebox, with lid, of any size

A pair of scissors

Green paint—enough to paint the inside of the box

A medium-sized paintbrush

Green tissue paper— enough to cover the lid of the box

A glue stick

Two or three handfuls of soil

Between five and ten small pebbles or rocks

Small pieces of plants

Sticky Tack

White paint

A thin paintbrush

One plastic tiger

Project: Three-dimensional collage

This art project is a collage made up of printed cut-outs made out of a variety of materials. The collage technique gives the picture a dynamic, three-dimensional appearance.

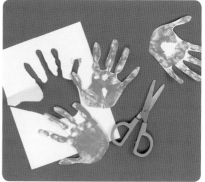

1 Wet the black paper all over with the sponge. Now paint in the stormy sky, covering the page with slanting diagonal strokes to create the effect of the rain. Let the paper dry.

2 Make handprints with the green poster paint on one of your sheets of white paper. The number you will need will depend on the size of the piece of black paper you are using. When the handprints are dry, carefully cut them out.

You will need

A sheet of strong black paper

A sponge

A medium-sized paintbrush

Poster paints in a variety of colors

A plate for mixing paints

About three sheets of white paper, any size

A pair of scissors

A selection of leaves

Pieces of broccoli

A thin paintbrush

A glue stick

3 On a clean sheet of paper make prints of the leaves in a red-orange color. Cut the broccoli in half and repeat the printing process with the broccoli in a contrasting color.

4 On a separate sheet of paper sketch out a tiger or trace Rousseau's tiger on page 58. Paint the tiger and allow it to dry. Cut out the tiger and the leaf and broccoli prints when they are dry.

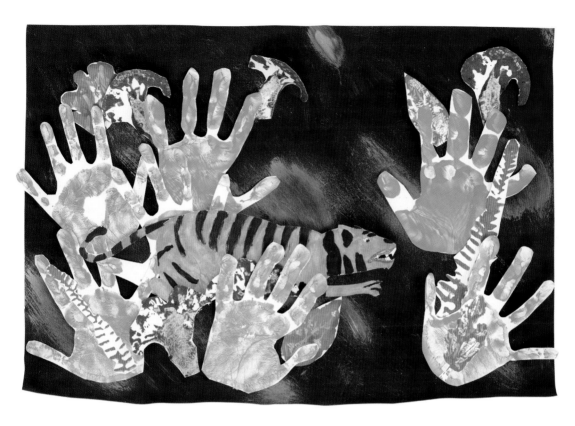

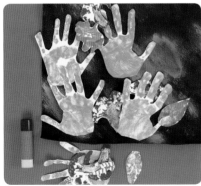

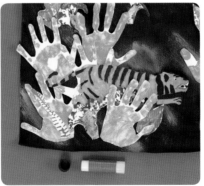

5 Arrange the prints on the paper with the broccoli representing the trees and the leaves and hands representing the plants and grasses.

6 Place the tiger in among your cut-out prints. Glue down all the pieces of paper when you are happy with your composition.

Top tips

- Clean your hands between using the different paint colors.
- Don't glue down the prints completely— leaving them free at the edges will give a more three-dimensional effect.

A Couple of Foxhounds

If you are lucky enough to own a pet you will know that sometimes we begin to think that our pets have human qualities and characteristics. Looking at George Stubbs's *A Couple of Foxhounds* you might think that these dogs were someone's beloved pets—not just two dogs taken from a hunting pack. Stubbs was so skilled that he was able to convey the character of these dogs and the almost human relationship between them. We can admire Stubbs's skill as a draftsman and his sensitive use of oil paints, but it is his ability to depict the character of these dogs that makes this painting special.

Artist	George Stubbs
Nationality	British
Painted	1792

What's the story?

Why was George Stubbs so good at painting animals? Probably because he knew his subjects inside-out—literally. Stubbs spent hours cutting open dead horses so that he could study how the muscles and skeleton looked and worked. His studies resulted in the publication in 1766 of *Anatomy of the Horse*, an illustrated book of his drawings and discoveries. This book brought him fame throughout Europe, not only because horses were the main method of transport so many people had one, but also because people recognized the quality and skill of his work. Wealthy people rushed to have their prize horses and animals painted by Stubbs.

Despite Stubbs's intense interest in his subject, he looked at whatever he was painting with cool detachment, setting the animals or figures in a perfectly composed natural-looking landscape. *A Couple of Foxhounds* was painted late in Stubbs's career as an artist and it brings together all the skills he had learned over all the years he had been painting. In it he demonstrates that he was one of the greatest artists of the 18th century.

Think about . . .

Why did Stubbs choose to show an imaginary landscape rather than a real one?
Stubbs wanted to bring out the best in the dogs so he created a landscape that showed off their beauty.

How did Stubbs manage to show the close relationship between the dogs?
Stubbs displayed his skill as a draftsman in his sensitive handling of the heads of the dogs—the position of their heads suggests a closeness and the male dog looks as though he is protecting the female.

"I think those dogs are friends.
They might even be married."

Jill, age 6

Project: Wall plaque

George Stubbs worked with the famous English potter Josiah Wedgwood. Stubbs painted a series of scenes of the countryside using delicate enamel colors on pottery plaques. This art activity uses the much simpler technique of painting on salt dough.

1 Combine all the ingredients needed for the salt dough in the mixing bowl. Knead for 10 minutes. Set aside in the fridge.

2 Trace around the dog shapes on page 65 or use your own designs. Cut out your trace of the dogs and transfer onto the cardboard or paper to make stencils.

Top tip

• Increase the quantity of salt dough according to the size of plaque you want to create.

• Add a tablespoon of vegetable oil to the salt dough to make kneading easier.

• Add a tablespoon of lemon juice to make the dough set harder at the finished stage.

3 Lightly flour your work surface and roll out half of the salt dough to approximately 8 x 7 inches (20 x 17.5 cm). Use a ruler to help you mark straight sides at the correct size. Cut out the rectangle.

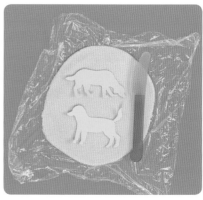

4 Now roll out the remaining dough, making sure that it's big enough for the two stencils to fit. Take your pencil and mark around the stencils. Lift off the stencils and cut out the dog shapes. You may need some adult help for this stage.

5 With the help of an adult, place the dough pieces onto a nonstick baking tray and put in the oven at 125°F (50°C) for 30 minutes and then increase the temperature to 212°F (100°C) for 3½–4 hours. Turn the dough pieces during this drying stage. Allow the dough to cool in the oven.

6 Paint the dogs and background. When the paint is dry, glue the dogs onto the rectangular piece of salt dough and then apply a coat of slightly watered-down white glue to give a nice shiny finish to your work.

You will need

To make salt dough mix 2 cups (100 g) of plain flour with 1 cup (250 g) of salt and 1 cup (250 ml) of water

Tracing paper

A pencil

Cardboard to make stencils

Flour for dusting

A rolling pin

A ruler

A knife to cut dough

A nonstick baking tray

Poster or watercolor paints

A paintbrush

White glue, watered down

Project: Stone paperweight

This activity is about making a stone paperweight showing a dog. You could make more paperweights showing other animals that fit the space, such as a curled up cat.

Top tip

• When painting your dog, allow each color to dry before adding another. This way you will stop the colors from running into each other.

• If you have difficulty finding a large smooth stone you could try going to a garden center or a hardware store to buy one.

You will need

A large stone, approximately 4 inches (10 cm) long, as smooth as possible

A selection of poster paints including black, brown, white, blue, and green

Medium-sized, thin, and thick paintbrushs

A pencil

Scratch paper

Enough white glue, watered down, to coat the stone

1 Wash and dry the stone so that it is clean. Do a sketch of a dog on the scratch paper. Paint the stone a light blue color all over, and let it dry. Add a dark brown area at the bottom where the dog will stand. Let the paint dry.

2 Lightly sketch your dog onto the stone.

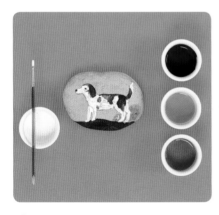

3 Paint in your dog using the poster paints. Add any other background details you want.

4 When the paint is dry, coat your stone with a layer of slightly watered-down white glue and let it dry—the glue will become see-through when it is dry and will give the painted stone a nice shine and a layer of protection.

5 Portraits

If you were asked what artists are trying to show in portraits, you would probably answer, "They try to capture the likeness of the sitter and maybe something of their character." But as you can see in this chapter, portraits are about much more than a straightforward likeness of a person. In the portrait of Queen Elizabeth I, a strong image of monarchy and power was presented to the people, and Amedeo Modigliani used the influence of African masks to create a masklike portrait.

The Rainbow Portrait

In order to understand this portrait, you have to put yourself into the minds of Queen Elizabeth I's subjects as they looked at the picture—they believed that God had given Elizabeth a divine right to rule, so she was seen as sacred. This portrait, known as *The Rainbow Portrait*, is not meant to tell us about Elizabeth, it is supposed to tell us about the power of the monarch. The artist has achieved this by putting a series of symbolic images into the picture.

Artist	unknown
Nationality	unknown
Painted	1600–1602

What's the story?

This portrait was painted between 1600 and 1602, and several artists have been credited with its creation. It was painted when Elizabeth was in her 60s (this was a very advanced age in the 17th century), so at once, we know that the artist was flattering the queen because she doesn't look over 60. But there was another reason that Elizabeth was portrayed so youthfully. It was believed that her virtue or goodness made her ageless. In her hand she holds a rainbow, and above it, there is a Latin inscription, *non sine sole iris*, which means "no rainbow without the sun." Elizabeth, resplendent in her golden orange dress, is the symbolic sun. It has been suggested that the rainbow is a reference to the story of Noah, in which the rainbow appears as a symbol of hope. The sun helps to make the rainbow, bringing hope to Elizabeth's subjects. On the sleeve of her gown is the serpent of wisdom, and on the rest of her dress, you can see eyes and ears to show that she sees and hears all that goes on in her kingdom. On her collar, there is a jeweled badge displaying her title *Fidei Densor*, which means "Defender of the Faith." On her head, she wears a headdress covered with jewels, and there are pearls around her neck. This portrait was a piece of propaganda, created to remind people of the might of their queen.

Think about ...

Is this picture a good portrait if it doesn't reveal anything about Elizabeth's character?
The artist never intended to show Elizabeth's character. He wanted to illustrate the majesty and power of Elizabeth as queen.

What is Elizabeth meant to represent?
Elizabeth is meant to be the sun bringing hope (represented by the rainbow) to her people.

Why does Elizabeth have a serpent on her sleeve and eyes and ears all over her dress?
These are all symbols of her queenship. People of the time would have recognized and understood these symbols.

NON SINE SOLE
IRIS.

Project: Oil painting

The art project inspired by *The Rainbow Portrait* has been spilt in two. The first activity recreates Elizabeth's portrait using homemade oil paints. In the second project you can make a frame for the portrait.

1 Start by lightly sketching in the outline of the portrait.

2 Mix up some flesh tones by adding a few drops of vegetable oil to the powder paints to make a creamy paste. Apply to the paper.

3 Now paint in the rest of the block colors. When the paint is dry, add in the details, including the rainbow and the gold highlights.

4 When the whole painting is dry, use the glue to stick down the pearl barley to represent Elizabeth's pearl necklace and the crystals for her jewels. Allow to dry. Now go on to the frame project.

Project: Frame

The frame of a royal portrait was very important. The frame would usually be carved from wood and then be covered in gold leaf (very thin sheets of real gold). For this project, we won't be using gold leaf but a mixture of dried pasta and pretend jewels on a wooden frame, painted gold.

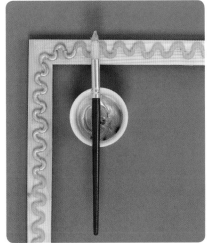

1 Arrange the pasta around the frame so that it forms a continuous pattern. When you are happy with your arrangement, glue the pasta down.

2 When the glue is dry, paint the frame and pasta in gold or silver.

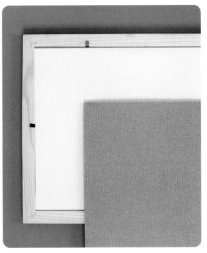

3 When the paint is dry, decorate with mini jewels. Glue the jewels down and let them dry.

4 Put your royal portrait inside the frame.

Top tips

• You don't just have to use a frame that is a rectangle. You could use something like an oval, which was very popular during the 17th century, but check that it fits your portrait.

• If you want to use this idea to frame a modern picture, then you can leave out the decoration and just paint the frame in a color that you think will match best with your picture.

Portrait of Anna Zborowska

We think of a normal portrait as being a likeness of an individual. But when we look at Amedeo Modigliani's portraits, they all seem to have the same characteristics—elongated faces, eyes, and lips, and curving limbs that give the sitter's bodies a sense of movement. Modigliani also tended to use mostly earthy colors, such as browns and yellows, so many of his pictures have the same tone. Yet, despite this repeated style, we get a very clear idea of the individual character of Anna Zborowska from her portrait. How did Modigliani achieve this, and why did he paint his portraits with such recognizable characteristics?

Artist	Amedeo Modigliani
Nationality	Italian
Painted	1917

What's the story?

Modigliani was born into a cultivated Jewish family in Livorno, Italy, in 1884. Encouraged by his mother in his art studies he moved to Florence, then Venice, and finally to Paris in 1906. In Paris he met a group of avant-garde artists, including Pablo Picasso and Constantin Brancusi, who looked beyond Western art for their inspiration. Brancusi introduced Modigliani to masks and sculpture of the Baule of Côte d'Ivoire, and this was to be one of the strongest influences on his art. If you look at this portrait, you can see that she has an oval, masklike face. In 1917 Modigliani met Leopold Zborowski, a Polish poet who became his art dealer. Zborowski championed Modigliani's work and commissioned a portrait of his wife, Anna Zborowska. The portrait displays all of Modigliani's trademarks; a simple composition, drawn with a few warm colors to create an intimate atmosphere. Anna's collar frames her face, and her hair sits like a cap on her head. But her face reveals nothing, creating an air of mystery. Modigliani depersonalized his portraits, but at the same time, he tried to paint the essence of things so that his art would reach beyond a particular time and place.

Think about . . .

Anna Zborowska's face looks like a mask. Was this intentional?
Yes, it was due to Modigliani's study of masks from Côte d'Ivoire in Africa.

If you painted this picture using bright colors, how would this change the painting?
Using bright colors would alter the whole mood of the painting. Bright colors would also change the balance of the painting as the outlines in the portrait would no longer dominate the picture. You might like to try this out yourself to see the difference it makes.

Project: Collage portrait

This art project recreates the *Portrait of Anna Zborowska* in the form of a collage using assorted papers including newspaper, brown paper, and magazine pages.

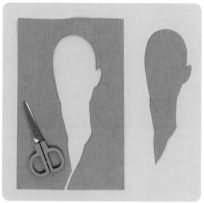

1 On the white paper, draw a line with your pencil that divides the paper in two columns. Find magazine pages similar to both the yellow and red sides of Modigliani's painting and tear them into long strips. Glue them into blocks on each side of the paper.

2 On the brown paper, draw and cut out Anna's face and neck. Then stick it down on top of the yellow and red collage background.

You will need

A sheet of white heavy paper, 11 x 17 inches

A pencil

A magazine

A glue stick

A sheet of brown paper

A pair of scissors

A sheet of black paper

A doily

A small piece of silver foil

Coloring pencils

4 Now cut out pieces of a doily to create Anna's collar and stick them around her neck and shoulders.

5 For the brooch, cut out an oval from a magazine page and stick it down. Take your silver foil and roll it to make a thin straw. Then stick it down to form the surround of the brooch.

3 Draw the shoulders on the black paper. Then cut out and stick them onto the collage paper, joining them up with the neck. Repeat this step for Anna's hair and place it a little way down her head.

6 Finally, sketch in the face and then color it in using your colored pencils.

Project: Shape a face

In this project, the *Portrait of Anna Zborowska* is recreated using a variety of paints and painting techniques. The paint is applied in stages. By working in this way, you will come to see how Anna's portrait was made up of a series of clearly defined shapes.

1 Begin by sketching an outline of Anna's portrait. Then paint in the background blocks of yellow and red and leave them to dry.

4 Using your fine paintbrush, paint in the flesh tones and the rest of the portrait in sections of plain colors. Allow to dry.

You will need

A sheet of 11 x 17 inches white heavy paper

A pencil

Poster or powder paints in similar colors to Anna's portrait

A thick paintbrush

Black watercolor paint or watery powder paint

A sponge

Containers to mix paint

A fine paintbrush

A sheet of black paper, larger than 11 x 17 inches

A glue stick

2 With a damp sponge, apply a layer of thin black watercolor paint to the background (the first layer of paint should still show through) and allow to dry.

3 Mix up a darker yellow to match the stripes in Anna's portrait and apply it to the yellow block with a dry brush so the paint is applied evenly. Allow to dry.

Top tips

• Take time to mix up the paint and get the right shade.
• When sketching out the portrait it helps to think of Anna's face as a series of clearly defined shapes, such as an oval for her head and a cylinder for her neck.
• Note the sharp outline of her face and neck.

5 Now add in the details such as the facial features and the light and shade. Allow the paint to dry between each application.

6 When the painting is dry, glue your finished painting onto a larger sheet of black paper to create a simple frame.

6 Landscape

The paintings chosen for this chapter give a very small sample of just how differently landscapes can be portrayed, both in terms of style and in the materials used. In Barent Avercamp's *Winter Landscape* there are many detailed figures at work and at play. In Paul Cézanne's picture, nature dominates in a haze of color, and in Whistler's painting, the buildings of Venice merge into the background, evoking a mysterious mood.

Winter Landscape

When we look at this landscape by Barent Avercamp we enter into his world. The painting's tiny dimensions and circular shape almost suggest that the scene is being viewed through a telescope. It is a closely observed world full of lively people enjoying winter activities.

Artist	Barent Avercamp
Nationality	Dutch
Painted	17th century

What's the story?

Barent Avercamp, like his uncle the artist Hendrick Avercamp, lived most of his life in Kampen in the Netherlands. It is believed that he studied and trained with his uncle. Indeed, Barent's paintings show such a close similarity to his uncle's that for many years they were attributed to Hendrick and not to him.

Like his uncle, Barent explored the same theme of winter landscapes featuring people at play. In addition to Barent's trademark detailed observation, what marks out this particular landscape is its size; it measures only a little more than 3 inches (8 cm) across, making it slightly smaller than the length of a playing card. This picture is called a medallion, and it was painted in oil paints on a wood panel. It is extraordinary how much detail Avercamp managed to pack into such a small area. The circular shape of the picture increases the illusion of perspective, giving the image an even greater sense of depth.

Avercamp painted a scene of a port. Ports were very important places to the Dutch because they were a great exploring and trading nation. Winters were much colder in the 17th century, causing rivers to freeze over for long periods of time, and so life was continued in all its aspects on the frozen ice. The figures at work and at play are painted in dark colors with splashes of red to enliven them. This kind of painting became very popular, possibly because it presented a world that was comfortable and happy, without any harsh realities.

Think about . . .

What effect does the circular shape of the painting have?
It gives the picture a greater sense of depth, producing a tunnel-like effect.

Why did Avercamp paint most of the figures in dark colors?
If he had painted them in lighter colors they would not stand out so clearly against the ice and a lot of the detail would have been lost.

Why did Avercamp set his painting in a port?
The Dutch were an important trading nation and so ports were very much a part of Dutch life.

"The people are so tiny they look like little insects. I like that boy's sled."

Lucy, age 10

Project: Snow jar

Have you ever wondered how they get the snow inside a snow globe? In this next project, you will discover how to do this so that you can create your own winter landscape.

1 Mold the Sticky Tack into a disk and put it in the bottom of the jar. The tack will represent the ice.

4 Pour the water into the jar and add about two teaspoons of glycerine and five teaspoons of glitter.

A screw-top jar with as wide an opening as possible

Sticky Tack

A sheet of 8½ x 11 inch (Letter) paper

A pencil

A piece of transparent plastic (the type that food containers are made from), not too thick

A black permanent marker

Acrylic paints

A fine paintbrush

A pair of scissors

Water

A teaspoon

Glycerine, available from the drugstore

Silver or white glitter

Clear tape

A rubber band

2 On your paper, draw a skating figure or whatever you want to choose from Avercamp's painting—remember that your picture needs to be small enough to fit in the jar. Put your plastic over the drawing and trace your drawing with the marker.

3 Paint your figures on the plastic and allow them to dry. Cut out the shapes, leaving a long strip at the top of the figures to attach them to the top of the jar.

5 Using tape, stick your cut-out figures onto the inside of the jar lid.

6 Screw the lid back on and secure with a tight rubber band. Shake to watch the snow fall.

Project: Medallion picture

In this art project, we are going to reproduce the content and format of Barent Avercamp's winter medallion picture. We will combine the colors used in the sky to add the figures and fine details throughout the rest of the painting.

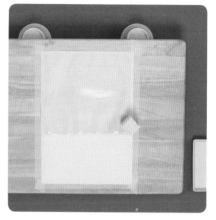

1 Mix the paint: make the yellow runny, the blue slightly thicker, and the gray thicker still. Tilt your board and use a sponge to cover two-thirds of the page with yellow paint, starting from the top.

4 Take a cotton ball and while the paint is still wet, dab and twist it over the clouds to give a fluffy appearance.

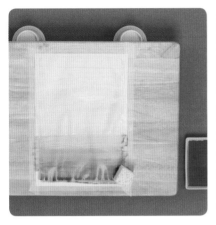

2 Using your other sponge, apply the blue color to the final third of the paper. The color will probably be darker at the bottom of the sheet because of the tilt of the board.

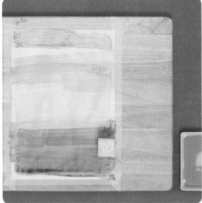

3 Lay the board flat and rinse out the blue sponge. Use it to apply the gray paint to make thick clouds in random streaks all over the sheet.

5 Mix all three colors together in a small container. When the sky is dry, place your plate in the center and draw around it with your pencil. Using the combined color, paint the figures and other details inside the circle.

6 To make a simple frame, take the folded black piece of paper, which, when folded, needs to be the same size as your picture, and use the plate to make a circle in the middle. Cut out the circle. Fit in your picture.

You will need

White heavy paper, any size, stuck with masking tape to a board

Powder paint in yellow, blue, and gray

Two sponges

Cotton ball

A small container to mix up the three colors of paint

A thin paintbrush

A plate to act as a circle guide

A pencil

Black paper, the same size as the white paper when folded

A pair of scissors

Top tips

• It is important to work quickly when painting the sky, to finish before the paint dries.
• On a spare piece of paper, make some sketches of the buildings and figures you are going to draw.

Mont Sainte-Victoire

Some of the artists in this book, such as Caravaggio (see page 120), were noted as geniuses from the moment they picked up a paintbrush, but not even Cézanne's closest friends saw any talent in his early work, and it was dismissed as unimportant. For Cézanne, art was a continual struggle to try to express and understand the relationship between forms (the way that objects look next to each other).

Artist	Paul Cézanne
Nationality	French
Painted	c.1904–1906

What's the story?

Cézanne's early attempts at painting were an effort to understand the nature of forms. It was one of Cézanne's friends, the Impressionist painter Camille Pissarro, who showed him Impressionist painting techniques that allowed Cézanne to explore the effects of light in pictures. But ultimately Cézanne came to the conclusion that capturing an impression was not what he wanted to do in his pictures because he worked too slowly. Cézanne decided that his art was about recording his feelings while he was standing in front of nature. "There are no straight lines in nature," he said. "Straight lines are imposed by the artist." Cézanne then worked at depicting a three-dimensional world on a two-dimensional canvas. "The main thing in a picture is to achieve distance. I try to render perspective solely by means of color." This is what we see Cézanne doing in *Mont Sainte-Victoire*—he built up layers of color in planes and modeled objects with color to give the scene a three-dimensional appearance. Color is the unifying force that seamlessly brings together the other elements of Cézanne's composition and forms the picture into one harmonious whole. Cézanne tried to paint the essence of an object, such as what makes a tree look like a tree, so that he could capture a moment suspended in time.

Think about . . .

The colors seem blurred together. Was this intentional?
Yes, for Cézanne colors were a unifying force that held all other elements in a painting together.

The Impressionists' paintings were also blurred. Was Cézanne also trying to capture an impression?
Cézanne was not trying to capture a fleeting moment but trying to reveal the true essence of the subject he was painting.

The painting's composition seems very simple. Was there a reason for this?
By breaking his composition down into simple forms, Cézanne hoped to reveal all of the relationships between them.

Project: Box sculpture

Cézanne believed that artists should draw and paint nature by the cylinder, the sphere, and the cone with everything in proper perspective, so that each side of an object is directed toward a central point. This sculpture is all about making shapes, the importance of shape in a composition, and how this creates a sense of the landscape.

1 Choose a box as your main structure—preferably a rectangular box with a top-opening lid. Cut off the corners of the remaining boxes to make triangular pieces and set aside.

2 Reshape the box—press it down so the sides buckle, lift the lid, and squeeze a corner. Cut a diagonal down one side, repeat on the other side, and extend the cut. Then twist the box around. Tape the box together with masking tape, so that it holds its new shape.

3 Arrange the triangular pieces around the main box, and when you are happy with the arrangement, glue them on and cover all the joints with tape.

4 When the glue is dry, paint your sculpture using a different shade for each surface. This will emphasize all the different angles of the planes.

You will need

An assortment of empty boxes

A pair of scissors

Masking tape

White glue

Acrylic paints in similar shades to Cézanne's painting

A medium paintbrush

Top tips

• Once you have completed one sculpture, go on to experiment with different shapes.
• Test out colors on a piece of scratch paper to ensure you have the color you want.
• You can achieve a different look depending on the colors you use. Use contrasting colors, like black and white, or complementary colors, such as red and green.
• If you don't have any acrylic paints, just add white glue to poster paint.

Project: Watercolor picture

When you look
at Cézanne's oil
painting, the first
thing that strikes
you is how blurred
the image appears.
Using watercolors
can produce a
similar blending of
colors, but to give
the painting the
more solid quality
that oil paints have,
we are going to
cover our watercolor
with salt, in order to
add a textured finish.

1 Roughly sketch out the most important features of Cézanne's painting on your paper.

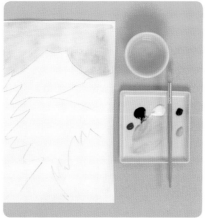

2 Spread water across the paper with the damp sponge until the whole page is covered. Begin painting, starting with the sky and color it with the palest color you can find.

You will need

A sheet of 11 x 17 inch white watercolor or heavy paper

A pencil

A damp sponge

Watercolor paints in similar shades to Cézanne's painting

A medium paintbrush

Salt

3 Fill in the rest of the background, building up the color from the palest to the darkest. Block in the foreground last.

4 When the painting is complete, and before it has dried, generously sprinkle the salt all over the paper and allow it to dry. When the picture is dry, shake off the excess salt.

Top tips

• Don't make the paper too wet.
• Work quickly while the paper is still wet.
• Have a scratch piece of paper handy to test new colors. This will help you be sure you are happy with the shade.
• Once you have finished you may need to flatten the paper with some heavy books and leave overnight.

Nocturne in Blue and Silver

In *Nocturne in Blue and Sliver*, Whistler did not set out to record an accurate picture of the city of Venice. A clue to his intentions lies in the title of the painting. The word nocturne is a musical term that describes a short lyrical piece of music. But the word nocturnal means "of the night," and this is the Venice that Whistler painted. The city emerges through the mist, its lights twinkling seductively, floating like a phantom on the dark water.

Artist	James Abbott McNeill Whistler
Nationality	American
Painted	1879–1880

What's the story?

James Abbott McNeill Whistler was born in America but spent most of his life in Europe. Whistler went to Venice for practical reasons. In London in 1878, he was involved in a libel case against the art critic John Ruskin. Although Whistler won the court case, he was awarded only a farthing (a quarter of a penny) in damages so he had to declare himself bankrupt. The following year, he was commissioned by the London Arts Society to produce a series of prints of Venice. He stayed in Venice for 15 months, living in cheap accommodation, having to borrow art materials from other artists. He produced over 50 etchings, 90 pastels, and 3 oil paintings, of which the *Nocturne* is one.

In the composition and lines of the *Nocturne,* you can see the influence of Japanese art, which was being seen and collected in Europe for the first time. For Whistler, painting was about creating beauty that would "improve on nature." But it was the way Whistler put paint onto canvas that marked him as an influential painter; he applied paint with the utmost delicacy, or as Whistler himself put it, "Paint should not be applied thickly. It should be like a breath on the surface of a pane of glass."

Think about . . .

Why are the buildings of Venice difficult to see?
Because Whistler wanted to paint a mood, not buildings.

What mood did Whistler create in the painting?
A mood of mystery and of an otherworldliness.

How did Whistler create his intended mood?
He applied the paint with a very delicate touch and surrounded the city with a mist. We are only aware of the buildings because of their twinkling lights, shining through the half light.

"I think there are pirates in that picture. You can see their ship."

Jordan, age 9

Project: Misty scene

In this project, the moonlit city of Venice is captured using dark blue paper and a stencil of the city's silhouetted horizon. These elements are combined with a paint-splattering technique that uses an old toothbrush. The finer details are then added after the stencil has been lifted. The paint splattering can be messy, so be sure to cover yourself and your work area before you start.

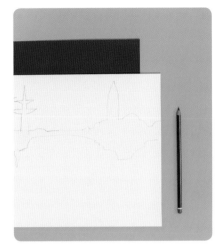

A sheet of thin white poster board or heavy paper, 11 x 17 inches

A pencil

A pair of scissors

A sheet of dark blue construction paper, 11 x 17 inches

Masking tape

Poster or powder paints in pale shades

An old toothbrush

A ruler

Gold or yellow poster or powder paint

1 Draw the silhouetted objects from Whistler's painting onto the white poster board.

2 Cut the horizon out. Place the cut-out shapes onto the colored paper. Secure with masking tape.

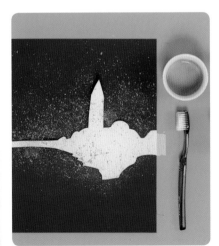

3 Make sure the paint is runny. Put the toothbrush in the paint and draw a ruler over the bristles toward you. The paint will splatter away from you. Repeat with another color.

4 When the paint is dry, carefully lift off the cut-out shapes and add details to the buildings. Highlight the reflections on the water with gold or yellow paint.

Top tips

• Don't overload your toothbrush with paint or it will drip.
• Clean your toothbrush between using different colors.

Project: Japanese painting

Nocturne in Blue and Silver clearly shows the influence of Japanese art in its technique and composition. Japanese artists use rice paper and colored inks, but we will use textured paper and watercolor paints in this project.

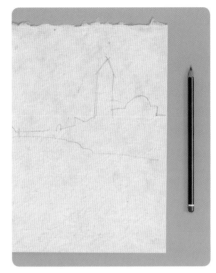

A sheet of textured white paper, 11 x 17 inches

A pencil

Watercolor paints

A medium paintbrush

Gold acrylic paint

1 Sketch out the horizon of Venice on your white paper.

2 Fill in the silhouettes with black watercolor paint.

3 Gradually build up the other colors using an almost-dry paintbrush.

4 Finally, add the highlights with gold acrylic paint and allow the picture to dry.

Top tip

Remember to use an almost dry paintbrush because the paper might bubble if it gets too wet.

7 Myths & legends

Why have artists through the ages chosen to paint
scenes from myths and legends? Probably because
myths and legends are filled with exciting plots
and superhuman characters so artists can let their
imaginations run wild. Paolo Uccello coolly and
elegantly portrayed St. George and the dragon, yet we
are still drawn to the drama of the scene. The artist
who painted the *Head of the Medusa* captured the full
horror of the moment.

St. George and the Dragon

In *St. George and the Dragon* Paolo Uccello created a fantastical and decorative world. The figures are elegant, the circles on the dragon's wings and the squares of grass make beautiful patterns. This picture is quite clearly of its time, both in its subject matter and in the costume of the figures, yet it is just as interesting to modern eyes as it was when it was first seen.

Artist	Paolo Uccello
Nationality	Italian
Painted	c.1470

What's the story?

St. George and the Dragon was painted toward the end of Uccello's life. The picture was based on a story from *The Golden Legend*, a collection of stories on the lives of the saints. The painting depicts two scenes from St. George's story: the point at which St. George defeats the dragon and the princess is rescued, and also the moment when he uses the princess's belt to tie up the dragon in order to take it into the town. The gathering storm clouds indicate that St. George has the support of divine forces. The focus point of the painting is the tip of St. George's lance as it pierces the dragon. The knight's lance cuts through the picture in a sharp diagonal—in fact, it is the only straight line in the painting. The rest of the picture is composed of curves, spirals, and patterns. The wonderfully undulating horse, with his spiraling tail, is mirrored in the dragon's tail. The colors are cool, except for the carefully balanced use of red. But perhaps the most fantasy-like features of all are the figures of St. George and the princess. Despite St. George's charge against the dragon, they both give off an air of serenity. As for the two-legged dragon, it is hard to believe that this is a beast that terrified a town. He looks more like the princess's tame pet on a leash. Uccello created a magical world that we are fascinated to enter, ensuring that this painting is as appealing to people now as it was when it was created, 500 years ago.

Think about . . .

The painting is mainly composed of cool colors, such as blues and grays, except for some splashes of red. Why?
The cool colors lend a detached, almost dreamlike mood to the painting. The use of red highlights the cool colors further and adds to the decorative elements within the painting.

The painting has lots of curvy and spiraling shapes. Why?
In addition to producing a decorative effect, the spirals put movement into the painting and direct our attention toward the contrasting shape of St. George's straight lance.

"I know the dragon is on a leash, but I think he is still scary because of his teeth and all that dripping blood."

Rosie, age 11

Project: Dragon story box

This art project takes its inspiration from the story of St. George and the dragon, from *The Golden Legend*. There are two scenes from the story in Uccello's painting, but, in this project, you will be able to incorporate the entire story in a specially made box. Read the storyboard on page 109 to find out the whole story of St. George and the dragon.

Read the storyboard on page 109 to find out the whole story of St. George and the dragon.

You will need

A small box with a lid approximately 2 x 2 inches (5 cm) square

Decorative jewels

White glue

A strip of pale-colored construction paper or heavy paper the same width as the box and about 12 inches (30 cm) long

A pencil

Some coloring pencils or felt-tip pens

A glue stick

1 Decide on a design for the lid of your box; this could be the dragon, St. George, the princess, or simply a pattern. Sketch in your design, color in the lid, and stick on some decoration using white glue.

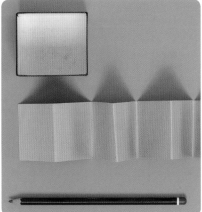

2 Fold your strip of paper into an accordion pattern of squares or rectangles that will fit inside the box. If you follow the measurements given, you should end up with about seven squares with a ½ inch (1.25 cm) of paper left over, which needs to be on the left.

Storyboard

- A country is terrorized by a dragon.
- The dragon is given two sheep a day to eat.
- When the sheep run out, a raffle is drawn for people to be given to the dragon.
- One day the king's daughter is selected.
- The king is allowed seven days until his daughter has to be taken to the dragon.
- As the princess approaches the dragon's cave, St. George appears.
- St. George makes the sign of the cross and "smites" the dragon.
- Using the princess's belt, St. George ties up the dragon. The princess leads it back to the city.
- St. George tells the people that he will kill the dragon if they are baptized.
- A church of St. George is founded. It has a holy well.

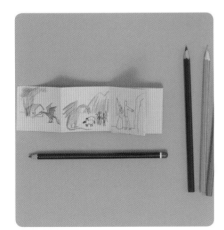

3 Decide which part(s) of the story you want to depict. Sketch in the episodes of the story, square by square, working from left to right. Then color in your pictures.

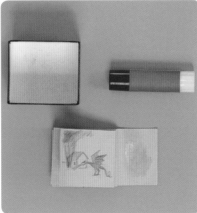

4 Use a glue stick to attach the extra ½ inch (1.25 cm) piece of the story strip to the inside bottom of the box. Fold down the strip and close the box lid.

Project: Mosaic dragon

This next art project is inspired by the ancient art of *tesserae* or mosaic, where small colored pieces of glass, tile, or stone are set into a floor or wall to make wonderful pictures and patterns. In this project, we are going to use paper to create a mosaic dragon.

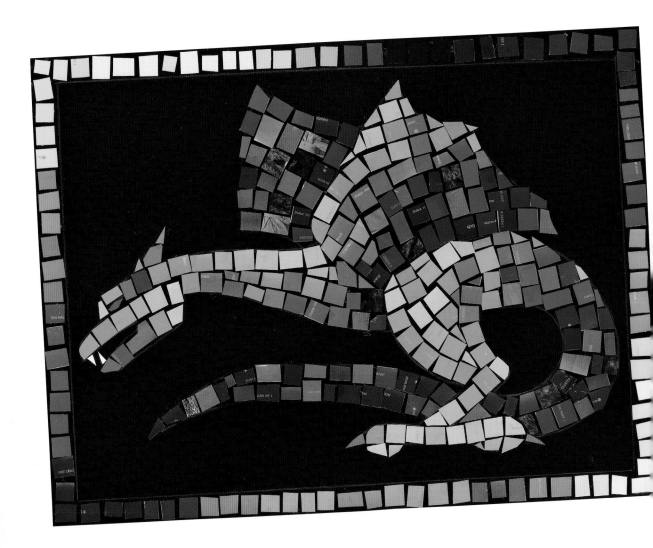

You will need

A pencil

Black construction paper, 11 x 17 inches

A ruler

Colored paper, old magazines, paint sample color strips, or tape

A pair of scissors

White glue

A medium paintbrush

A small household paintbrush

1 With your pencil, draw a dragon onto the construction paper. Draw a border all the way around the picture with your ruler.

2 Cut up your colored paper into ½-inch (1.25-cm) squares and divide them into piles of the same colors.

3 Glue the squares onto the paper inside the drawing/border. Leave gaps so that they look like tiles.

4 Mix some white glue with water. Paint all over the mosaic to make it shiny. Allow your picture to dry.

Top tips

• If using paint color sample strips, you could use the same color in different shades. This will give your mosaic more of a three-dimensional feel.
• You could also try using colored foil or wallpaper.

Head of the Medusa

The story of Medusa from Greek mythology is one that has fascinated artists throughout the centuries. Artists from Caravaggio to Rubens have used Medusa as a subject for their paintings. This Medusa is now attributed to the Flemish school (c.1620–1630), but for centuries it was thought to be by the artist Leonardo da Vinci. So what makes this version of Medusa so special?

Artist	Flemish School
Nationality	Flemish
Painted	c.1620–1630

What's the story?

In Greek mythology, Medusa was a daughter of the sea gods Phorcys and Ceto. Medusa was a mortal woman whom Athena (goddess of wisdom, war, and the arts) changed into a gorgon. Gorgons were vicious female monsters with brass hands, sharp fangs, and living venomous snakes for hair. Anyone looking upon Medusa's face would be turned into stone. Medusa was killed by Perseus, one of the first Greek warrior heroes. He then presented her head to Athena, who placed it on her shield.

The viewpoint of this painting of Medusa is very unusual. Instead of the more common image showing her whole face from the front, Medusa's head is lying on the ground, and we are immediately confronted by a mass of writhing snakes. To add to the drama of the moment, the artist used extreme effects of light and shade, allowing just a slither of light to fall onto one side of her face. A mist comes out of Medusa's open mouth that surrounds her whole head. Through the mist we can seen toads, bats, and other sinister creatures. Despite the writhing snakes, we feel sympathy for Medusa. Her face is plainly human in its obvious fear. We are drawn into her nightmare and share her horror of it. This is what makes this painting and its interpretation of the Medusa story unique.

Think about . . .

Why did the artist show Medusa from an inverted angle?
So that we are immediately confronted by the writhing snakes, adding to the drama.

What effect does the mist have on the mood of the painting?
Things seem to loom out at us through the mist, giving a sinister mood to the painting.

The artist surrounded Medusa with toads, bats, and other creatures. Why?
The other creatures make us aware that Medusa is being observed, and they reinforce the horror of her situation.

"I think all those snakes are really scary."

Scott, age 10

Project: Medusa mask

Make your own Medusa mask using a balloon, papier mâché, garden wire, and bubble wrap.

1 Blow up the balloon to roughly the size of your head. Then tie a knot in it. Mix the wallpaper paste. Tear the newspaper into small strips. Mix with the paste and then cover half the balloon. Add another layer. Then allow it to dry. Repeat until you have built up about eight layers of papier mâché.

4 Paint the face and allow it to dry. With the craft needles make pairs of holes around the edge of the mask (just above the forehead) where the hair will go. Cut lengths of garden wire with the pliers.

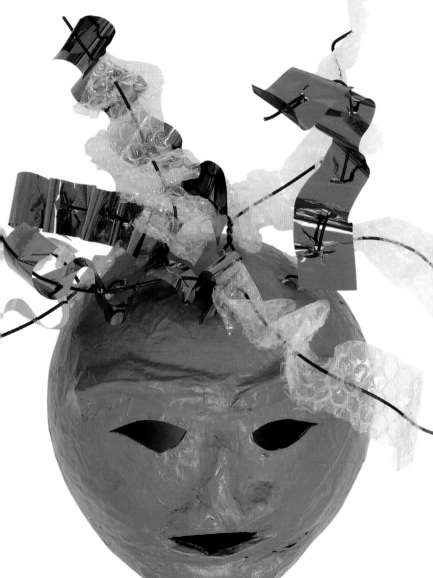

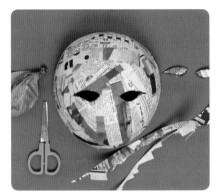

2 Allow the papier mâché to dry out completely, and then pop the balloon to remove it. Trim the edges of the mask, and make eye holes and a mouth with a pair of scissors.

3 Draw the rest of the facial features with a pencil. Scrunch up small pieces of newspaper and stick them on with masking tape to form the nose, eyebrows, chin, and mouth. Add two layers of papier mâché and allow to dry.

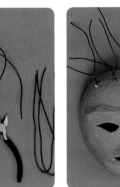

5 Thread a length of wire through each pair of holes. Twist the wires together just above the holes to keep them in place. Bend the wires into snake shapes, then weave them each through a strip of bubble wrap or shiny foil.

6 Repeat this step with all the other holes and wires. Alternate the materials between bubble wrap and shiny foil. Secure each of the wire ends with clear tape to avoid poking.

You will need

A balloon

Wallpaper paste

Newspaper

A broad paintbrush

A pair of scissors

A pencil

Masking tape

Poster paints

A medium paintbrush

A craft needle

Garden wire, the type used for tying up plants

A pair of pliers

Strips of bubble wrap and shiny foil

Clear tape

TOP tips

• Vary the lengths of wire you use for the hair.
• Candy wrappers are a good source of different colors of foil.

Project: Monochrome Medusa

This next art project uses black construction paper and white string to recreate Medusa's head in black and white.

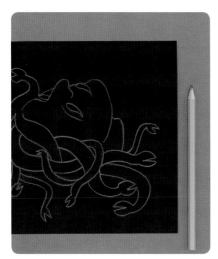

1 Sketch an outline of Medusa's face, neck, and hair of snakes.

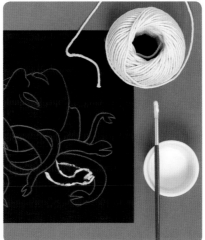

2 Paint the white glue over a section of the pencil lines.

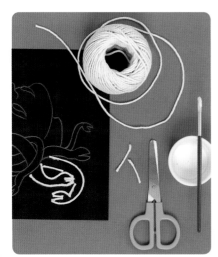

3 Measure bits of string and cut. Stick them down over the glue lines. Try to use long pieces rather than lots of small pieces. Repeat steps 2 and 3 until all the pencil lines have been covered.

4 Cover your work with a sheet of greaseproof paper and weigh it down with some heavy books. Leave overnight. When completely dry, mount the head onto a sheet of white paper.

You will need

A sheet of black construction paper, 11 x 17 inches

A pencil

White glue

A fine paintbrush

A ball of white string

Scissors

Greaseproof paper large enough to cover the construction paper

A sheet of white paper larger than the construction paper

A glue stick

Top tip

Don't make your sketch too elaborate—the simpler the better.

8 Light & shade

How do light and shade play a big part in the composition, mood and drama of a painting? If you look at the extreme, theatrical light used by Caravaggio in *The Supper at Emmaus* and the vibrant, contrasting tones in Franz Marc's *Im Regen (Under the Rain)*, you will get some idea of how artists express emotions using effects of light and shade in their paintings.

The Supper at Emmaus

Caravaggio's painting has a tremendous dramatic force. *The Supper at Emmaus* shows the moment of revelation when Christ's identity is revealed to the apostles sitting with him. Yet, despite the Christian subject matter of this work, the church was Caravaggio's fiercest critic. So what was it that made Caravaggio's art so controversial?

Artist	Michelangelo Merisi da Caravaggio
Nationality	Italian
Painted	1596–1602

What's the story?

Caravaggio's life was as dramatic as his paintings. His terrible temper led to him being continually on the run to escape prison. Caravaggio painted in a style that matched his personality. He painted straight onto the canvas with very little preparation and quickly painted over work he didn't like. Caravaggio introduced a revolutionary realism to art that was shocking in its directness. The apostles were painted as ordinary working men. Only Christ's gesture of blessing reveals his identity. It was this ordinariness that drew such criticism from the church.

One of the painting's greatest strengths is the way that we are drawn into the action of the scene. The innkeeper looks puzzled by the reactions of the apostles, but we know the secret. Such is the shock created by Christ revealing his identity that it cannot be contained in the space of the picture, but erupts out from the canvas. St. Luke broadly gestures as he recognizes the hand of Christ. St. Matthew's elbow bursts from his jacket. The fruit bowl balances precariously on the table's edge. But perhaps the real scene-stealer in the painting is the light. Caravaggio used light in his paintings in a theatrical way. Christ's shadow reinforces his blessing gesture so that the light in the painting is like the light of truth revealing Christ. Caravaggio transformed the ordinary into the extraordinary, and this is what makes him one of the greatest artists of the 17th century.

Think about . . .

What emotions did Caravaggio try to capture?
Caravaggio wanted to capture the wonder, surprise, and shock of the apostles at the exact moment that they realize Christ is sitting at the table with them.

How did Caravaggio heighten the drama of the scene?
Caravaggio used extremes of light and shade and contrasted the dramatic gestures of the apostles with the calmness of Christ. He also stretched the natural perspective of the painting, e.g., the jutting elbow, and he let us in on Christ's secret. We are not puzzled by the apostles' reactions, unlike the innkeeper.

"If that's Jesus, then he looks pretty normal in this picture. Just like anyone really."

Bruce, age 11

Project: Fabulous fruit

This art project focuses on the wonderful still life of the fruit in a bowl that balances precariously at the edge of the table in Caravaggio's painting. You feel that you could reach out and pluck the fruit from the bowl. Such was Caravaggio's skill at making the fruit appear real. We are going to make our own fruit with a combination of paper, glue, and paint.

1 Start by scrunching up your newspaper into different shapes of fruit, any size you want.

2 Tape around the fruit to hold the shapes in place.

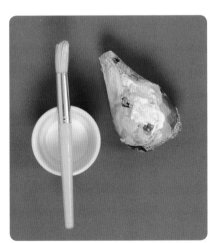

3 Make a mixture of watered-down white glue and brush it onto the fruit. Allow the glue to dry.

4 Paint your fruit. Build up the colors and allow them to dry between coats. Put on another layer of watered-down glue. Allow to dry. Cut the pipe cleaners to fit. Then push in as stalks.

Top tip

The fruit could be used in the next project as props for the still life sketch in pencil.

Project: Sight drawing

The next art project is all about observing—using your eyes to really look at things. We are going to focus on the still life of the bowl of fruit that is a key feature of Caravaggio's painting. We are going to use the fruits from the previous art project, but if you have not yet made these, you can of course use real fruit. Artists use all sorts of materials for their sketches—pencil, charcoal, graphite. By using monochrome you will come to understand how a composition is held together and also how light and shade help to add depth and drama to a picture.

1 Start by creating a display: select your fruit and arrange it. Add props if you like, such as a plate, napkin, or knife.

2 Select a 2B pencil. Place your display on a table a few feet away and lightly sketch its outline.

You will need

The 3-D fruit from the previous project or fresh fruit

Any other props required, such as a plate, knife, or napkin

Some sheets of mid-tone printer or construction paper in cream or gray, 8½ x 11 inches (Letter) or larger

A selection of pencils ranging from 2B to 6B

A piece of chalkw

3 Once you are confident you have drawn the basic shape of the fruit, start filling in the details. Look for the darkest areas first, and observe if your still life casts a shadow on the surrounding surfaces. Take care to shade the darkest areas in with the highest number B pencil.

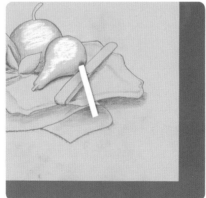

4 Once the dark areas are shaded in, start filling in the lightest areas using the chalk.

Top tips

• When you draw more than one object, you need to consider and compare their proportions.
• Do lots of sketches from different angles and in different kinds of light.
• To achieve a greater contrast between the light and the shadows, you could switch on a desk lamp above your still life.

Im Regen (Under the Rain)

Have you ever noticed how the rain changes the colors in the landscape? The rain often seems to make colors appear softer and less intense. But in Franz Marc's *Im Regen* (*Under the Rain*), the weather has created a tropical world inhabited by strange people and animals. As the rain falls, the colors glow with intensity and the contrast between light and shade deepens.

Artist	Franz Marc
Nationality	German
Painted	1912

What's the story?

Franz Marc was born in Germany in 1880 and studied at the Munich Academy of Fine Arts. He traveled to Paris where he was influenced by the work of Vincent van Gogh and Paul Gauguin. He returned to Germany, and, in Berlin, along with Wassily Kandinsky and August Macke, he formed a breakaway art group called the Der Blaue Reiter (the Blue Rider), named after a painting by Kandinsky of a blue rider on a blue horse. The group printed their new ideas about art in *Der Blaue Reiter Almanac* and held influential exhibitions that invited artists of many different modern styles to come together to show their work to the public.

For the Blue Rider artists, art was powerful only if it directly expressed feelings. Marc was influenced by the modern art styles of Futurism (an Italian art movement interested in the depiction of speed, machines, movement, and modern life) and Cubism (a French art movement that broke down everyday objects and then put them back together again in a slightly disjointed way to represent an object from lots of different angles), but at the heart of his work was the wish to reveal the spirituality of nature. Marc expressed this spirituality through color. For Marc, colors represented emotions: blue stood for masculinity and spirituality, yellow was femininity and joy, and red represented the sound of violence.

Think about . . .

Why did Marc call this painting *Under the Rain*?
The title gives Marc the opportunity to show contrasts, such as the driving rain against the bright colors and the strong diagonals against rounded shapes.

Why did Marc use such vibrant colors?
For Marc, color was a means of expressing emotion, with each color representing a different feeling.

If you had to choose colors to express different moods and emotions, what would those colors be and what would they express?
This is entirely your choice. You may like to put down your ideas in another art project.

"I think the red lady is very pretty. Is that her dog?"

Beth, age 9

Project: Giant flowers

This project tries to capture the vibrant colors of Marc's painting by creating a tropical setting. If you have ever been to a rainforest or seen pictures of one you will know that everything appears larger than life and very lush. These flowers are set against a stormy sky so that their colors appear even more intense.

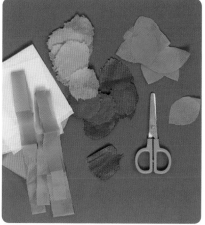

You will need

A sheet of 11 x 17 inch white heavy paper

A damp sponge

Watercolor paint or watered-down powder paint in blue-gray tones

A paintbrush

Tissue paper in shades of pink, red, orange, and green

A pair of scissors

A glue stick

A fine black felt-tip pen

1 With a damp sponge apply a thin layer of moisture all over the sheet of paper. With your paintbrush add gray watercolor paint in broad sweeping strokes.

2 While the paint is drying, tear or cut up the pink, red, orange, and green tissue paper into petal, stem, and leaf shapes.

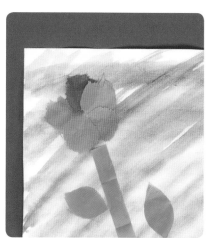

3 Arrange the petals, stems, and leaves on the dry sheet. Layer and overlap the tissue petals. Then glue all the tissue pieces down.

4 Make sure the glue is dry. Then take your fine felt-tip pen and add detail to the flowers and leaves.

Top tips

• The more you layer and overlap the tissue, the more effective the flowers will look.

• When you are gluing down the petals, don't glue them down completely. This will give a more three-dimensional effect.

Project: Futurist scene

This project captures the Futurist style of Marc's work, as well as the hot, intense colors he used in *Im Regen*. To recreate these elements all you need is some old magazines. The effect of the driving rain can be made by cutting up the pictures and setting them in diagonals.

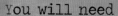

You will need

Some old magazines, particularly ones that feature landscapes, people, and animals

A pair of scissors

A pencil

A ruler

A sheet of 11 x 17 inch white heavy paper

A glue stick

A piece of black construction paper bigger than your finished picture

1 Select some suitable pictures from the magazines.

2 Cut out your chosen pictures in long thin strips. You may want to use a pencil and a ruler.

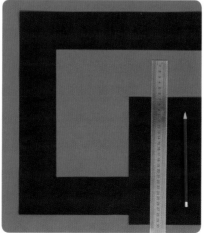

3 Arrange the strips in diagonals onto the white paper. When you are happy with your arrangement, glue down the strips, making sure that there are no gaps.

4 When the glue has dried, make a simple frame for the picture using some black construction paper or any other black paper.

Top tips

• Take time to arrange the paper strips to get a good balance of colors.
• Don't worry if you can't get similar animals or people to Marc's painting. The idea is just to get the feel of bright colors shifting and moving.

Artist biographies

Barent Avercamp

1612/13–1679

Dutch

Barent Avercamp was the nephew of Hendrick Avercamp (1585–1634), a famous Dutch artist who specialized in depicting winter landscapes. Barent was probably taught to paint by Hendrick, and for a long time, paintings signed with "Avercamp," or "B. Avercamp," were thought to be by Hendrick, but now, any paintings with either of these signatures, or thought to be painted after 1634 (the year of Hendrick's death), are attributed to Barent. Barent was a merchant, as well as an artist, and, like his uncle, he painted landscapes.

Michelangelo Merisi da Caravaggio

1571–1610

Italian

Caravaggio was an Italian artist. He lived a short and controversial life. But his paintings have influenced generations of artists. His paintings were startlingly realistic to his contemporaries, who were used to the exaggerated forms and compositions of Mannerism, the dominant artistic style of the time. Caravaggio painted characters and scenes from Classical myths and legends, as well as saints and stories from the Bible. He used ordinary people as models for his paintings, so his figures from Christianity look just as ugly, unhealthy, or unattractive as everyone else, not idealized and perfect as they were in most paintings of the day. Caravaggio used dramatic light in his paintings. He shifted from bright, illuminating light to areas of dense shadow and darkness very suddenly, with no transitional areas of diminishing light in between. These lighting effects make his paintings emotional, exciting, and full of action.

Caravaggio was notorious for his drunken brawling and irresponsible lifestyle, and in 1606, he killed a man during a fight and then fled Rome (the scene of his crime). He spent the next four years on the run, in and out of prison, and getting into fights in many places. The exact details of his death are unknown, but it is thought that he died of a fever at a port in Tuscany. He was on his way to seek a pardon for his crimes. He was 38 at the time of his death, and his body has never been found.

Paul Cézanne

1839–1906

French

Paul Cézanne was a Post-Impressionist painter. This means that he was painting after the Impressionists, and he took the Impressionist style a step further in its development. Cézanne's style of art inspired and influenced the next generation of painters, called the Cubists. He is credited with creating a bridge in painting between the 19th and 20th centuries.

Cézanne was interested in painting the truest elements of nature. He tried to break down the forms of mountains, fields, and trees into planes, lines, circles, spheres, and blocks of color that would reflect their essence. In this way, he hoped that he could make art that would have permanent significance and would be hung in art galleries for many years. Cézanne's technique of painting nature was a direct inspiration for Pablo Picasso and Georges Braque, the founders of Cubism, the first major art movement of the 20th century.

Theo van Doesburg

1883–1931

Dutch

Theo van Doesburg was a Dutch architect, poet, decorator, and painter who founded the De Stijl art movement in 1917. Several artists, including Piet Mondrian

(1872–1944) and Bart van der Leck (1876–1958), grouped together to publish a magazine that told people about their views on art; the magazine was called De Stijl ("the style" in Dutch) and soon the art movement itself was known by the same name. De Stijl artists believed that art was about more than representing the world around us—they thought that it should be a spiritual experience. De Stijl artists thought that the only way art could be spiritual was for it to mirror the harmony and order of math—so only squares, rectangles, and horizontal and vertical straight lines were used and only pure primary (red, yellow, and blue) colors and black and white were allowed. De Stijl artists wanted their paintings to be very disciplined. De Stijl art was abstract, which means it did not represent the world in a realistic way. Van Doesburg was the leading member of De Stijl and he traveled to Germany to visit the Bauhaus, the most influential art and design school in Europe at the time, to promote De Stijl's ideas.

Albrecht Dürer

1471–1528

German

Dürer was one of the most important artists in Western art thanks to the huge number of works he created, his thriving print business—which meant that his art was seen all over Europe—and his many skills and talents. He was a woodblock artist, a painter, printmaker, and a writer on art, math, and perspective.

Flemish school

15th and 16th centuries

Flanders

Artists who were working in the Low Countries or Flanders, from the middle of the 15th century onward.

The Low Countries was the name given to the modern-day countries of Belgium, Luxembourg, and the Netherlands. Flanders is an area now within modern-day Belgium. Artists from this part of Europe usually worked in or around the two main cities of Bruges and Ghent. Art of the Flemish school came to prominence at the same time as the Renaissance in Italy (15th century), and famous artists of this school include Jan van Eyck and Hugo van der Goes.

Lipunja

dates unknown

Aboriginal Australian

We know very little about Lipunja, other than the fact that this artist was working in Arnhem Land, Australia, in the 1960s.

Kazimir Malevich

1879–1935

Russian

Kazimir Malevich studied at the Moscow Institute of Painting, Sculpture, and Architecture from 1904–10. In 1913 Malevich saw Cubist works for the first time, was greatly influenced by them, and began painting in a Cubist style. In 1915 Malevich created his own style of art, which he called Suprematism. Suprematism was a truly Russian art movement and was based on geometric shapes, such as squares and circles, painted in starkly contrasting colors, such as a black square floating on a white background, or a black circle floating on a white background.

Franz Marc

1880–1916

German

Marc was a German Expressionist painter and, along with August Macke and Wassily Kandinsky, a founding member of the Der Blaue Reiter (the Blue Rider), a group dedicated to expressing new ideas and attitudes toward modern art. Marc liked to depict animals and he made woodcuts and lithographs as well as paintings. His work made use of bright, primary colors, which he believed had emotional properties that communicated through the artwork. Marc was drafted into the German army during World War I and was killed in action in 1916.

Henri Matisse

1869–1954

French

Henri Matisse was a lawyer who turned to painting after his mother bought him a set of paints to amuse himself while recovering from appendicitis. Matisse went on to become one of the greatest artists of the 20th century. Matisse was not only a painter, but also a sculptor and printmaker. He is best known for his bold and expressive use of bright colors and flowing drawing style. As a young man Matisse was a founding member of a group of artists called the Fauves, which means "wild beasts" in French. These artists used bright, unmixed colors in a bold and energetic style to express their emotions. One of Matisse's most famous Fauvist paintings is *Woman with a Hat* (1905). With time, Matisse became more and more respected, producing a great deal of work between 1906 and 1917 as part of the Paris avant-garde art scene. After 1917 Matisse moved outside Paris and continued to create a vast quantity of work right up until his death in 1954 at the age of 84.

Amedeo Modigliani

1884–1920

Italian

Modigliani was born into a Jewish family in Livorno, Italy, in 1884 and suffered bad health, particularly tuberculosis, as a child. He trained as an artist in Italy and then moved to France, where he spent the rest of his working life. Modigliani painted and sculpted in a Post-Impressionist style and made a great many portraits. His work was influenced by the art of non-Western cultures, such as Cambodia and West Africa. Modigliani died of poverty and tubercular meningitis at the age of 35.

Henri Rousseau

1844–1910

French

Henri Rousseau worked as a customs officer for most of his life and taught himself to paint. At the age of 49 he gave up his work and concentrated on painting. Rousseau's paintings are called naïve or primitive because they seem quite childlike but they are actually very complex and skilled. Rousseau's landscapes have a magical atmosphere, possibly because he made a lot of his pictures up—he painted pictures of jungles but he had never been to a jungle. Rousseau didn't receive approval from art critics during his lifetime but he influenced the next generation of artists, including Pablo Picasso.

Jakob van der Schley

1715–1779

Dutch

Jakob van der Schley was born in Amsterdam in 1715 and was trained by French engraver Bernard Picart, who greatly influenced his style. Very little is known about his life and career but we do know that he worked as a draftsman and engraver in Amsterdam. A small number of engravings, illustrated books, maps, and portraits by van der Schley have survived in private and public collections.

Georges Seurat

1859–1891

French

Georges Seurat invented a new style of painting called Pointillism, or Divisionism, where tiny dots of color are painted next to each other which, from a distance, take on the appearance of different colors. Seurat based his painting style on scientific color theories that were popular at the time. He painted *A Sunday Afternoon on the Island of La Grande Jatte* in his Pointillist style—it measures 10 feet (3 m) across and took him two years to complete—it has become one of the most famous pictures of the 20th century.

George Stubbs

1724–1806

English

Stubbs was born in Liverpool, England. Between 1745 and 1751 he made a living painting portraits in the north of England and in his spare time he studied anatomy at York County hospital. Stubbs studied horses in great detail, spending 18 months dissecting them and drawing every aspect of them. Stubbs was a meticulous artist, obsessed by understanding anatomy as a means of perfecting his art. Stubbs worked for wealthy people who kept horses and packs of hunting dogs and wanted a record of their ownership of the animals. Stubbs also painted lions, tigers, and monkeys.

Paolo Uccello

1397–1475

Italian

Paolo Uccello was a mathematician as well as an artist, and this can be seen in his work, which always grappled with the mathematical problems of perspective related to painting. Uccello was not a very prolific artist, painting only a few large commissions in his lifetime. His most famous works are the three battle scenes he painted depicting the battle of San Romano. In those pictures, soldiers and horses are set out on a strict perspective grid.

James Abbott McNeill Whistler

1834–1903

American

Whistler was born in Lowell, Massachusetts, and attended the West Point Military Academy. He learned drawing and mapmaking from Robert W. Weir, the historical painter and a member of the Hudson River School of American art. After leaving West Point, Whistler worked as a draftsman, drawing the US coastline for the military. In 1855, Whistler decided to become a painter, and he traveled to Paris where he took a studio, studied art, got into debt, and met the painters Edouard Manet, Gustave Courbet, and Theophile Gautier, as well as the writer Charles Baudelaire. In 1859, Whistler moved to London, which was to be his home for the rest of his life. He now perfected his painting style, working on pictures with a limited range of colors, which gave his compositions an overall tonal harmony. He attempted to paint the harmony that is present in music. Whistler was also influenced by the composition of Japanese prints. His most famous picture is *Arrangement in Gray and Black: The Artist's Mother,* also known as *Whistler's Mother,* and it can be seen in the Musée d'Orsay in Paris.

Glossary

A

Abstract: A picture that doesn't look anything like objects or people in the world. Many art movements of the 20th century were abstract and a lot of today's art is abstract.

Avant-garde: Innovative art at the forefront of the development of modern art.

B

Baroque: A style of art that depicts scenes from the Bible and Classical mythology in a very bold and heroic way. Baroque paintings can be large in scale and use rich colors, including gold, to communicate the drama and emotion of a scene. The baroque style of art flourished from the late 16th century to the early 18th century. Sir Peter Paul Rubens (1577–1640) painted in the baroque style.

Brancusi, Constantin (1876–1957): Brancusi was a Romanian artist who lived and worked in Paris as a sculptor. Brancusi concentrated on paring down his sculptures of objects, people, and animals into simple and elegant shapes that represented the essence of the subject he was tackling. Some of his most famous sculptures are the group known as *Bird in Space*, sculpted throughout his life and *The Kiss* (1916).

C

Chevreul, Michel Eugène: A chemist who had a keen interest in restoring tapestries. Chevreul noted that when he filled in a bare patch on a tapestry he had to take into consideration the color of the wool surrounding the bare patch. He discovered that if he sewed certain colors of wool next to each other they looked like a different color from a distance. From

this he formulated the color wheel, which shows the complementary color of every color. Artists were very interested in Chevreul's theories and the Pointillists used them in their work.

Composition: The arrangement of elements in a picture such as line, color and form.

Collage: A way of constructing art in which the piece is assembled using different materials, objects, and shapes.

Cubism: An art critic, Louis Vauxcelles, named the Cubist movement by noticing that Cubist pictures were "full of little cubes." The first phase of Cubism was called Analytical Cubism and it was active between 1908 and 1912. In Analytical Cubism paintings everyday objects were broken down into basic shapes, taken apart, and put back together again in a slightly disjointed way to represent an object from lots of different angles at the same time. The second phase of Cubism took place between 1912 and 1919 and was called Synthetic Cubism. Synthetic Cubism incorporated collage–bits of newspapers, fabric, magazines, and books–into pictures. Synthetic Cubism stuck objects together, rather than pulled them apart.

D

De Stijl: Dutch for "the Style," was an art movement that originated in the Netherlands in 1917 and it was active until around 1931. De Stijl artists believed that art was about more than representing the world around us–it was a spiritual experience. De Stijl artists thought that the only way art could represent the spiritual was for it to mirror the harmony and order of math–so only squares, rectangles, and horizontal and vertical straight lines were used and only pure primary colors (red, yellow, and blue) and black and white were allowed. De

Stijl art was abstract, which means it did not represent the world in a realistic way. In addition to painters there were De Stijl architects, poets, writers, and even furniture makers.

E

École des Beaux-Arts: The name given to a collection of famous art schools in France, the most well-known of which is in Paris. Many of France's most accomplished artists trained there, including Edgar Degas, Claude Monet, and Georges Seurat.

Engraver: Someone who produces engravings. Engraving, or etching, is a way of making a picture on paper with ink that can be copied many times. The image is cut with acid into a sheet of copper metal, called a plate. The plate is then covered in ink and the ink wiped off. The ink stays in the lines that have been cut into the plate. A damp sheet of paper is then placed on top of the plate and the plate and paper are put into a press. The ink in the cuts is transferred to the damp paper while it is pressed, producing a print.

F

Futurism: An Italian art movement of the early 20th century that produced paintings, sculptures, textiles, ceramics, interior design, literature, architecture, music, and industrial design. The Futurists were led by Filippo Tommaso Marinetti (1876–1944), a writer who laid out the principles of the movement in the *Futurist Manifesto*, first published in 1909. The Futurists hated the art of the past and were interested in all of the wonders of the modern industrial age, such as speed, machines, airplanes, cars, and motorcycles. The Futurists believed that youth and violence should be praised above all the achievements of the past.

G

Gauguin, Paul (1848–1903): One of the most influential and important Post-Impressionist painters, Paul Gauguin was a French artist who produced oil paintings, drawings, woodcuts, and engravings. Gauguin was influenced by Impressionism—he knew Camille Pissarro (1830–1903), Paul Cézanne (1839–1906), and Vincent van Gogh (1853–90)—but felt that it was too superficial a style. Gauguin's work was more symbolic than the Impressionists' work and he was further influenced by folk art, Japanese art, and West and Central African art. In 1891, Gauguin traveled to Tahiti and Polynesia where he painted local people and landscapes until his death there in 1903.

German Expressionism: Several movements in art, architecture, theater, music, and cinema that emanated from Germany in the 1920s and 1930s form the German Expressionist movement. Expressionism tried to communicate the essence of being alive, both emotionally and physically, rather than exactly reproducing what things looked like.

J

Japanese prints: Woodblock prints from Japan were imported into Europe in large numbers during the 19th century. These prints influenced European artists who copied their compositions and use of color and line. Other Japanese arts and crafts, such as porcelain, ivory carving, silk, and furniture, also influenced artists, photographers, and designers.

K

Kandinsky, Wassily (1866–1944): Russian artist who is widely acknowledged as the first painter to create completely abstract works of art. An abstract picture doesn't look anything like objects, people, or things. Kandinsky was a cofounder of the Blue Rider group, taught at the Bauhaus, an influential German art school, formulated theories about the emotional and physical significance of colors, and analyzed elements of paintings, such as the point and the line.

L

Leonardo da Vinci (1452–1519): An Italian artist, scientist, inventor, writer, poet, sculptor, botanist, engineer, and musician. Many people think that Leonardo da Vinci was the greatest artist of the Renaissance because his interests spanned the arts and sciences and his accomplishments ranged from drawing to plans for weapons of war, such as the helicopter and the tank, to painting masterpieces such as *The Last Supper* (1498) and the *Mona Lisa* (1503–05/07).

M

Macke, August (1887–1914): A German Expressionist painter and a member of the Blue Rider group along with Wassily Kandinsky. Macke was influenced by Impressionism, Cubism, and Futurism. He was killed in World War I, at the age of 27.

Mannerist: Artwork that reflects Mannerism, a style of art that flourished in Europe, particularly in Italy, from about 1520 to 1580. Mannerism wasn't interested in depicting people, landscapes, plants, and animals in as realistic a way as possible but instead it showed these things in elongated forms, under dramatic lighting and with lapses in perspective and scale. Mannerists used these techniques to represent the world in a way which they thought was more elegant and perfectly beautiful than the art which had gone before.

Modern: The word modern is often used to describe any artwork, style, or movement that moves away from classical and traditional forms. When people say "modern art" or "modern architecture," they often simply mean things that were created in the 20th century or later. However, the terms "Modernist" or "Modernism" usually refer to a particular development in Western art and literature that began in the late 19th century and lasted until the 1950s and '60s. Modernists deliberately rejected the styles of the past and celebrated innovation and experimentation to better reflect the realities of their daily lives.

N

Neo-Plasticism: Another name for the De Stijl art movement.

P

Patron: Someone who employs artists such as painters, sculptors, composers, and musicians.

Perspective: The skill of being able to draw or paint an object on a two-dimensional surface, such as a piece of paper, so that it looks three-dimensional. During the Renaissance, artists worked out mathematical formulas for perspective.

Picasso, Pablo (1881–1973): A Spanish painter and sculptor who is widely accepted as the greatest artist of the 20th century. Picasso cofounded Cubism with Georges Braque and pioneered abstract painting.

Pisarro, Camille (1830–1903): A French painter who was an important follower of Impressionism and is significant in his role as a mentor to the important Post-Impressionist artists Paul Cézanne (1839–1906) and Paul Gauguin (1848–1903).

Pointillism: A style of painting developed by the Post-Impressionist painter Georges Seurat. Pointillism was a painstaking style of painting that involved placing tiny dots of color next to each other so that from a distance the paint takes on the appearance of an entirely different color.

R

Realist: A style of painting that originated in France in the 19th century. It aimed to depict exactly what the artist had seen. The Realists painted ordinary things, such as rural life and working people, rather than famous people, incidents from history, Classical mythology, or scenes from the Bible. The Realists painted in a rough style, applying the paint in a way that was meant to indicate that they had seen the thing they were depicting, rather than being restricted to working in a studio.

Rubens, Sir Peter Paul (1577–1640): A Flemish painter who created work in the Baroque style, but was also an academic and a diplomat. Rubens painted religious subjects, portraits of European royalty, self-portraits, scenes from Classical mythology, and stories and incidents from the Bible in a dramatic and energetic style. Rubens ran a large workshop of apprentices who finished works he drew. Rubens also created tapestries and prints.

S

Suprematism: A short-lived Russian art movement founded in 1915 by Kazimir Malevich. Suprematism was based on geometric shapes, such as squares and circles, painted in starkly contrasting colors, such as a black square floating on a white background, or a black circle floating on a white background. Suprematism became less popular in the 1920s but influenced later Russian art movements.

V

van Gogh, Vincent (1853–90): A troubled Dutch Post-Impressionist painter, famous for his bouts of mental illness, for cutting off a part of his left ear, for having a volatile friendship with Paul Gauguin, and for his lack of success during his lifetime. Van Gogh taught himself to paint and sometimes worked at a furious pace, creating a work a day toward the end of his life. Van Gogh committed suicide at the age of 37.

where to see the art in this book

Henri Matisse, *The Snail*, Tate Gallery, London, UK

Georges Seurat, *The Circus*, Musée d'Orsay, Paris, France

Albrecht Dürer, *Portrait of Bernhard von Reesen*, Gemäldegalerie Alte Meister, Dresden, Germany

Jakob Van der Schley, *Buffel, Buffle*, Buffalo Bill Historical Center, Cody, Wyoming, USA

Theo van Doesburg, *Composition in Gray*, Peggy Guggenheim Collection, Venice, Italy

Kazimir Malevich, *Suprematist Composition*, Peggy Guggenheim Collection, Venice, Italy

Henri Rousseau, *Surprised!*, National Gallery, London, UK

George Stubbs, *A Couple of Foxhounds*, Tate Gallery, London, UK

Unknown artist, *The Rainbow Portrait*, Hatfield House, England, UK

Amedeo Modigliani, *Portrait of Anna Zborowska*, Galleria d'Arte Moderna, Milan, Italy

Barent Avercamp, *Winter Landscape*, Hamburger Kunsthalle, Hamburg, Germany

Paul Cézanne, *Mont Sainte-Victoire*, Detroit Institute of Arts, Detroit, USA

James Abbott McNeill Whistler, *Nocturne in Blue and Silver*, Museum of Fine Arts, Boston, USA

Paolo Uccello, *St. George and the Dragon*, National Gallery, London, UK

Flemish school, *Head of Medusa*, Galleria degli Uffizi, Florence, Italy (opposite)

Michelangelo Merisi da Caravaggio, *The Supper at Emmaus*, National Gallery, London, UK

Franz Marc, *Im Regen (Under the Rain)*, Städtische Galerie im Lenbachhaus, Munich, Germany

The location of Lipunja's bark painting is unknown.

Notes on materials

To make the most out of the activities in this book, some pointers regarding preparation and supplies are listed below:

- All of the art supplies listed in the activities should be easily obtainable from grocery stores, art and hobby shops, and hardware outlets. However, if you are having difficulty sourcing anything, the Internet has a wealth of retailers that can deliver supplies directly to your house.

- It is advisable to cover the area in which you are working with a waterproof sheet before you start any art activity. Remember to wash your tools and clean up your work area after the activity is over.

- It is a good idea to cover up in an old T-shirt or apron before activities get messy.

- If you can, try to use good-quality materials (such as brushes and paints) over poor-quality ones; you'll notice that it makes a big difference to the result of your art project, and good-quality materials are usually easier to work with.

- When buying brushes for any of the painting projects featured in the book, please note that brushes are numbered according to size: the smaller the number, the finer the brush.

- For media like watercolors, use two bowls of water to rinse your brushes so that the next color you use is not affected by the previous one.

- White glue is used throughout this book, because it is water soluble and dries well. It is available from many suppliers and is sometimes called school glue. A mix of one part water to two parts glue will create a shiny varnish that can be painted over your work to seal it in place.

Index

First published in the United States of America in 2017
by Chicago Review Press Incorporated
814 North Franklin Street
Chicago, Illinois 60610
ISBN 978-0-912777-04-7

Conceived and produced by
Elwin Street Productions Limited
14 Clerkenwell Green
London EC1R 0DP
www.elwinstreet.com

The activities described in this book are to be carried out with parental supervision at all times. Every effort has been made
to ensure the safety of the activities detailed. Neither the author nor the publishers shall be liable or responsible for any
harm or damage done allegedly arising from any information or suggestion in this book.

Library of Congress Cataloging-In-Publication Data
Names: Pitamic, Maja, author. | Laidlaw, Jill A., author.
Title: Fine art adventures : 36 creative, hands-on, projects
inspired
   by classic masterpieces/ Maja Pitamic and Jill
   Laidlaw ; introduction by Mike Norris, Metropolitan Museum of Art, USA.
Description: Chicago : Chicago Review Press, 2017. | Includes index.
Identifiers: LCCN 2016054105 | ISBN 9780912777047
Subjects: LCSH: Art appreciation--Juvenile literature. | Creative
activities and
   seat work--Juvenile literature.
Classification: LCC N7440 .P58 2017 | DDC 701/.18--dc23 LC record
available at https://lccn.loc.gov/2016054105

Cover design: Rebecca Lown
Cover layout: Elwin Street Productions Limited
Original Photography: Ian Garlick

Printed in China.
5 4 3 2 1